What Can I Do Now?

Safety and Security

Second Edition

D1224027

Books in the
What Can I Do Now? Series

What Can I Do Now?

Safety and Security

Second Edition

Ferguson
An imprint of Infobase Publishing

What Can I Do Now? Safety and Security, Second Edition

Ferguson
An imprint of Infobase Publishing
132 West 31st Street
New York NY 10001

ISBN-10: 0-8160-6030-4
ISBN-13: 978-0-8160-6030-6

Library of Congress Cataloging-in-Publication Data

What can I do now? Safety and security.—2nd ed.
    p. cm.
  Includes index.
  ISBN 0-8160-6030-4 (hc ; alk. paper)
  1. Law enforcement—Vocational guidance—United States. 2. Police—Vocational guidance—United States. 3. Emergency medical services—Vocational guidance—United States. 4. Fire prevention—Vocational guidance—United States. 5. Private security services—Vocational guidance—United States. I. J.G. Ferguson Publishing Company. II. Title: Safety and security.
  HV8143.W45 2007
  363.1023'73—dc22   2006031303

Text design by Kerry Casey
Cover design by Takeshi Takehashi

Printed in the United States of America

VB Hermitage 10 9 8 7 6 5 4 3 2 1

This book is printed on acid-free paper.

Contents

Introduction

If you are considering a career in safety and security—which presumably you are since you're reading this book—you must realize that the better informed you are from the start, the better your chances of having a successful, satisfying career.

There is absolutely no reason to wait until you get out of high school to "get serious" about a career. That doesn't mean you have to make a firm, undying commitment right now. Indeed, one of the biggest fears most people face at some point (sometimes more than once) is choosing the right career. Frankly, many people don't "choose" at all. They take a job because they need one, and all of a sudden 10 years have gone by and they wonder why they're stuck doing something they hate. Don't be one of those people! You have the opportunity right now—while you're still in high school and still relatively unencumbered with major adult responsibilities—to explore, to experience, to try out a work path or several paths if you're one of those over-achieving types. Wouldn't you really rather find out sooner than later that you're not cut out to be an FBI agent after all, that you'd actually prefer to be a fire-fighter? Or a corrections officer?

There are many ways to explore the field of safety and security. What we've tried to do in this book is give you an idea of some of your options. Section 1, What Do I Need to Know?, will give you an overview of the field—a little history, where it's at today, and promises of the future; as well as a breakdown of its structure—how it's organized—and a glimpse of some of its many career options.

Section 2, Careers, includes 10 chapters, each describing in detail a specific safety and security career: border patrol agent, corrections officer, crime analyst, emergency medical technician, FBI agent, federal aviation security worker, firefighter, fire inspector and investigator, police officer, and Secret Service special agent. These chapters rely heavily on first-hand accounts from real people on the job. They'll tell you what skills you need, what personal qualities you have to have, what the ups and downs of the jobs are. You'll also find out about educational requirements—including specific high school and college classes—advancement possibilities, related jobs, salary ranges, and the employment outlook.

Section 3, Do It Yourself, urges you to take charge and start your own programs and activities where none exist—school, community, or the nation.

The real meat of the book is in Section 4, What Can I Do Right Now? This is where you get busy and do something. The chapter "Get Involved" will clue you in on the obvious volunteer and intern positions, the not-so-obvious summer camps and summer college study, and other opportunities.

While the best way to explore public safety is to jump right in and start doing it, there are plenty of other ways to get into the public safety mind-set. "Surf the Web" offers you a short, annotated list of Web sites where you can explore everything from job listings (so you can start getting an idea of what employers are looking for now) to educational requirements to on-the-job accounts from those who keep the public safe.

"Read a Book" is an annotated bibliography of books (some new, some old) and periodicals. If you're even remotely considering a career in safety and security, reading a few books and checking out a few magazines is the easiest thing you can do. Don't stop with our list. Ask your librarian to point you to more materials. Keep reading!

"Ask for Money" is a sampling of safety- and security-related scholarships and other financial aid. You need to be familiar with these because you're going to need money for school. You have to actively pursue scholarships; no one is going to come up to you one day and present you with a check because you're such a wonderful student. Applying for scholarships is work. It takes effort. And it must be done right, and often as much as a year in advance of when you need the money.

"Look to the Pros" is the final chapter. It lists professional organizations you can turn to for more information about accredited schools, education requirements, career descriptions, salary information, job listings, scholarships, and more. Once you become a student in the safety and security field, you'll be able to join many of these. Time after time, professionals say that membership and active participation in a professional organization is one of the best ways to network (make valuable contacts) and gain recognition in your field.

High school can be a lot of fun. There are dances and football games; maybe you're in band or play a sport. Or maybe you hate school and are just biding your time until you graduate. Whoever you are, take a minute and try to imagine your life five years from now. Ten years from now. Where will you be? What will you be doing? Whether you realize it or not, how you choose to spend your time now—studying, playing, watching TV, working at a fast-food restaurant, hanging out—will have an impact on your future. Take a look at how you're spending your time now and ask yourself, "Where is this getting me?" If you can't come up with an answer, the response is probably "nowhere." The choice is yours. No one is going to take you by the hand and lead you in the "right" direction. It's up to you. It's your life. You can do something about it right now!

SECTION 1

What Do I Need to Know About the Safety and Security Industry?

Turn your television on right now, flip through the channels, and chances are you'll see at least one show featuring police officers, firefighters, criminal profilers, or federal investigators. The abundance of this type of program reveals our national fascination with the people who devote their careers to keeping the rest of us safe from harm. Maybe you've watched lots of these shows and are pretty sure you've got a handle on what the field of safety and security is all about.

Well, think again. The career possibilities are much more complex and—in many instances—exciting than what you might see portrayed on television. In the real world of safety and security, you'll discover jobs that you didn't even know existed. You'll also find that "tough guy" stereotypes of these workers are shattered. There are sentimental border patrol agents, giggly crime analysts, petite women working as corrections officers, and firefighters with master's degrees in English.

Certain things, however, hold true across the board: All of the careers described in this book require street smarts, creativity, deep-rooted concern for humankind, and tolerance for some degree of physical danger. Many of these jobs hire people straight out of high school and conduct their own training programs or academies. Other jobs are ideal for students who plan on going to college and doing internships in the summer. Others require a two-year associate's degree. Most importantly, you can get involved in these jobs while you're still in high school. This book will give you a window into the many ways of pursuing your career—right now.

GENERAL INFORMATION

Virtually every aspect of your life involves policies, regulations, and laws that help to promote public safety. Think about it. The exterior of your house meets certain codes, or rules, so that it won't catch on fire easily. Every time you drive a car, you follow a number of rules so that you won't cause or get in an accident. Even your dog has to obey regulations, like leash laws.

Some people make the mistake of thinking of public safety and the rules that go with it as strictly modern concerns. They romanticize the past as a safer, gentler, lawless era. But the fact is that the protection of a group of people—from both outside and inside the group—has been a concern for a long time. You have to look back at our earliest societies' efforts at public safety to truly understand and appreciate where we are today. As these societies developed, it became clear that people would run wild unless certain rules of conduct were created. Some laws evolved from the common agreement of the group's members, while others were handed down by the group's leaders.

But making a law is not the same thing as enforcing it, and soon after the establishment of rules and laws, methods of enforcement sprang up. For a long time, enforcement simply meant punishment. Those who broke the laws were often ostracized or exiled from the group, subjected to corporal punishment, tortured, maimed, or even killed. Enforcement of the law was usually left to the society's leaders or rulers, in many cases through the soldiers who served in their armies. Often these armies also collected taxes from the population, and these funds were in turn used to maintain the army (and sometimes to line the ruler's pockets).

Eventually, more organized methods of public safety were developed. In England, for example, earlier law enforcement officials were considered servants of feudal lords, kings, and other rulers, and their duties revolved around protecting their masters' interests rather than ensuring the public safety. The more modern law enforcement officials, however, became directly responsible for protecting the people from crime and fire. In addition, they continued to collect taxes, and they were also often responsible for the maintenance and safety of public buildings, property, and other facilities. Colonial America followed in England's footsteps and adopted its system of law enforcement.

Cities grew larger during the eighteenth and nineteenth centuries, and the need arose for even more organized efforts. You can compare the situation to today's urban problems; larger cities often mean more crime, riots, and other disorders. The first modern police force was formed in 1829 in London. Cities in the United States organized police forces as well, beginning with New York in 1844. As the United States stretched across the continent, many states created state police forces to work with those in the cities and towns. Interstate

Fire Facts

- In 2005, there were 1,602,000 fires in the United States. More than 21,000 civilians and 80,000 firefighters were injured or died as a result of these fires.

- The deadliest fire and explosion in U.S. history occurred at the World Trade Center on September 11, 2001, as a result of terrorist attacks. Nearly 2,700 people lost their lives.

- In 2005, there were 1,136,650 firefighters working in 30,300 fire departments in the United States.

- Women made up 3.9 percent of firefighting and fire prevention occupations in 2003.

Source: National Fire Protection Association

crimes were placed under federal authority, and various agencies, including the U.S. Marshals Office, the Federal Bureau of Investigation, the Secret Service, the Internal Revenue Service, and the Customs Service (known today as U.S. Customs and Border Protection), were formed to enforce laws across various jurisdictions.

The punishment of criminals changed as well. Beginning in the eigteenth century, efforts were made to create punishments that were equal to the crime. To deter people from committing crimes, societies began to develop specific punishments for specific crimes. These newer penalties generally called for a period of incarceration. Jails and prisons, which had historically been used as temporary holding pens before more permanent punishments like exile or death, became an important feature of these new concepts of punishment. The new prisons hired guards to watch over the prisoners, bring them food, and prevent them from escaping. The first American jails appeared in the late eigtheenth and early nineteenth centuries.

Another feature of protecting the public safety was the detection, prevention, and solving of crimes. Police officers who specialized in these efforts became known as *detectives*. Much like today, their job was to examine evidence relating to a crime in an effort to catch the person or persons responsible. They were also vigilant in trying to prevent crimes or to catch criminals in the act. During the nineteenth century, the first private detectives and detective agencies appeared. These agencies not only worked to solve crimes against their clients, but also offered guard services for people and their property. Solving crimes also became more and more scientific. As early as 1780, a crime was solved when a suspected criminal's shoes were found to match footprints left at the scene of the crime. Toward the end of the nineteenth and the beginning of the twentieth centuries, modern forensic science techniques were developed. Methods were developed to link fingerprints, bullets and other weapons, hair, soil, and other physical evidence found at a crime scene to the crime and the criminal. Laboratories were constructed

that were devoted to this work. The Federal Bureau of Investigation's laboratory, established in the 1920s, became the largest and most famous crime laboratory in the world.

Intelligence operations, the collection and evaluation of information about one's rivals or enemies, have also been a part of history for a long time. Spies were often sent from one group into another to determine the other's strengths and weaknesses. By gaining information about their enemies, groups were better able to protect themselves from attack. Before long, government agencies began to use intelligence-gathering techniques. The Central Intelligence Agency became responsible for preserving the United States' international interests. The FBI was charged with maintaining the country's internal security. The U.S. Department of Homeland Security was created in 2002 to oversee and coordinate government efforts to prevent terrorist attacks, as well as to provide assistance in the aftermath of such attacks on American soil. (Agencies under its supervision also assist with relief during and after natural disasters, such as hurricanes, tornadoes, and earthquakes.) Each branch of the military services also operates intelligence forces. The many agencies often work together and with state and local law enforcement officials in preventing and solving crimes and other threats to the public safety.

Preserving and protecting people's safety—especially during emergency situations—extends beyond law enforcement. A major threat to safety has always been fire, and throughout history, people have

(continued on page 8)

Lingo to Learn

Adam codes Codes used by law enforcement officers during radio communications to describe types of calls. For example, A1 means arrest, A20 means assistance rendered, and A63 means pursuit.

cluster analysis A computerized analysis of where specific crimes are happening. Crime analysts use this tool to identify crime "hot spots."

contraband Any forbidden item that is in a prisoner's possession.

coyote Border patrol slang term for an alien smuggler.

crime pattern The occurrence of similar crimes in a defined geographic area.

crime series A crime pattern where there is reason to believe that the same suspect is responsible for the crimes.

intelligence analysis The study of relationships between people, organizations, and events. This applies to organized crime; conspiratorial acts, such as money laundering; crime rings, such as auto theft or child pornography; or other crimes of corruption.

investigative analysis The study of why a person is committing crimes of a serial nature.

iinewatch A routine activity in which border patrol officers patrol the border for would-be crossers and apprehend them.

MO: Modus operandi (mode of operation); the standard way, or pattern, in which a particular criminal commits a crime.

probable cause Information developed by an officer to give a reason to arrest, search, or stop and detain a person.

reasonable suspicion The reasons an officer believes a person should be stopped and detained.

shakedown A thorough search of an inmate's cell, conducted by corrections officers looking for contraband.

sign cutting A technique in which border patrol officers smooth the surface of sandy areas along areas used for illegal entries. When these sand traps are examined, they show footprints. Officers can follow the "signs" and apprehend the offenders.

special agent A government title for federal employees who investigate criminal violations.

surveillance Following, observing, or listening to people for the purpose of obtaining information about criminal activities.

wiretap Electronic surveillance over the telephone.

yard-out This means that it's time for the inmates to go to the yard for exercise. Corrections officers say "chow-out" when it's time for the inmates to eat and "shower-out" when it's time for showers.

worked together to protect themselves and their property from fire damage. When a fire broke out, volunteers used to form lines to pass water buckets to douse the fire. In 1736, Benjamin Franklin organized the first permanent fire brigade in Philadelphia. Many other cities soon began their own fire departments.

The Industrial Revolution brought more sophisticated equipment to fighting fires. Nevertheless, when a fire broke out in a city, the results were often devastating because of crowded conditions, poor building techniques, and inadequate water supplies. The Great Chicago Fire of 1871, for example, destroyed much of the city. Codes and regulations were eventually established for buildings that made them less likely to catch fire and spread the fire to other buildings. New techniques and tools like hydrants, extinguishers, and sprinkler systems made it easier to respond quickly and effectively. Firefighters became highly trained in firefighting techniques and skilled in emergency medical techniques.

Emergency medical technicians (EMTs) also began to play an integral role in public safety. In the past, people had to rely on their family, neighbors, and, if they were lucky, the town physician for prompt medical help during an emergency. Now EMTs working for both public agencies and private companies can respond in minutes to critical medical situations as varied as a car accident, a heart attack, and a premature baby's delivery.

Clearly, emergency and protective services involve the cooperation of almost everyone in a society. Politicians draft legislation intended to promote the public well-being and to prevent threats to individual and public safety. Many organizations, both governmental and private, act as inspectors and watchdogs to see that regulations and laws are obeyed. Industries are always concerned about the safety of both their employees and the products they make. Start paying attention to all of the rules and policies that help to keep you safe. In your home, your workplace, your streets, state, and country, you'll find innumerable measures that ensure your safety and well-being.

STRUCTURE OF THE INDUSTRY

By far, the greatest number of people in emergency and protective services are working at the local level. Almost every community has its own police department. In the smallest communities, a police department may have as few as one or two employees. In larger cities, the members of a police department may be divided into many divisions, each with its own area of the city to patrol. A police force may have specialized divisions, such as a narcotics squad to combat illegal drugs; a vice squad to fight rape, prostitution, and related crimes; a SWAT team that can be called upon in emergency situations; a hostage rescue team; and a bomb squad. Most police departments employ a military-style ranking system. Patrol officers may become detectives. Police officers may rise through the ranks to become sergeants, lieutenants, or even the chief of police for a community. Many other people provide support for a police department, from traffic and police clerks to forensic experts and polygraph examiners.

Other important areas of local law enforcement are probation and parole services, which work in cooperation with police departments to monitor individuals who have received court-supervised probation or who have been released on parole from a correctional facility.

Sheriff departments generally operate at the county level, and provide additional law enforcement efforts among the many communities in a single county. Almost every state operates its own state police department. These are often called "highway patrols" because one of their major responsibilities is to ensure the safety of the highways linking communities.

The U.S. Marshals service, part of the U.S. Department of Justice, is concerned with crimes that cross state lines. Interstate crimes, as they are called, may involve the transport of stolen vehicles and goods from one state to another. U.S. Marshals are responsible for tracking down wanted criminals and transporting prisoners. They also operate the Federal Witness Security Program and provide security for federal courts and judges.

Enforcement of federal laws is largely the responsibility of the Federal Bureau of Investigation. The FBI oversees more than 200 separate violations, including such federal crimes as kidnapping. A principal duty of the FBI is to investigate people and groups that might pose a threat to the internal security of the country. The Central Intelligence Agency is primarily concerned with matters of international security, monitoring world events as they relate to the safety and interests of the United States.

In response to the terrorist attacks of September 11, 2001, the Bush administration restructured many existing government agencies and created new agencies to improve security at U.S. borders, in U.S. airports, in dealing with travelers throughout the United States, and in making the entire country safer from chemical, biological, or technological attacks or other potential threats. The U.S. Department of Homeland Security was created by the Homeland Security Act of 2002 to address these issues. It employs 180,000 workers who work in one of four major directorates: Border and Transportation Security, Emergency Preparedness and Response, Science and Technology, and Information Analysis and Infrastructure Protection. Many major government agencies—such as the U.S. Customs Service, Transportation Security Administration, Federal Emergency Management Agency, Federal Computer Incident Response Center, Secret Service, and Coast Guard—were merged into this new agency.

There are many other agencies operating at the federal level, including the Drug Enforcement Agency and the Internal Revenue Service. Each agency oversees a particular jurisdiction, or responsibility, of the law. However, every agency provides support and cooperation to the others, and each also works closely with state and local law enforcement agencies when investigating crimes and apprehending criminals.

The incarceration and rehabilitation of suspected and convicted criminals also occurs at each of the local, state, and federal levels. Communities usually operate jails, which provide temporary housing for people awaiting trial or for convicted criminals awaiting sentencing to permanent prisons. The prison system operates minimum-, medium-, and maximum-security prisons, depending on the nature of the criminal and the crime. Special prisons house mentally ill prisoners or juvenile offenders. People convicted of federal crimes are generally sent to prisons operated by the federal government.

In addition to their most obvious responsibility of fighting fires, fire departments are often charged with the inspection of public and private facilities to ensure that fire codes are enforced. Fire department officials also investigate the causes of fires. Many private individuals and companies are also involved in fire prevention and protection efforts. People are specially trained for planning, designing, installing, and maintaining fire safety systems. Others work for insurance companies and ratings bureaus, evaluating and inspecting a building's fire protection, prevention, and resistance capabilities.

Emergency medical technicians (EMTs) are usually the first to respond to emergency situations. Whether employed by a hospital, police department, fire department, or private ambulance com-

pany, the EMT crew functions as a traveling arm of the emergency room. An EMT might be called out for virtually any situation that could be described as a medical crisis.

Security agencies and detective agencies work to ensure the public safety as well. Many provide such services as bodyguards, security systems, armed security guards, and private investigation services in order to prevent crimes against people and property. Many private companies also work within the correctional system—operating prisons, providing corrections officers, and offering other services. Some private companies also provide police and fire services for universities, communities, and large government facilities and installations.

CAREERS

There are literally hundreds of career options in the field of emergency and protective services. Below are descriptions of a handful of career possibilities, some of which will be explored in greater detail later in this book.

Police officers are responsible for protecting life and property in their community. They preserve the peace, prevent criminal acts, enforce the law, and arrest people who violate the law. Police officers are also charged with enforcing traffic regulations, directing traffic, and providing security and crowd control functions at public events. *State police officers* perform similar duties at the state level, and also enforce the laws and regulations governing the use of highways. Police officers are often confronted with dangerous situations, so they must have maturity, bravery, emotional control, and the ability to think clearly and act quickly in times of stress.

Detectives are police officers who almost always work in plainclothes. They are responsible for investigating crimes, pursuing suspects, and building evidence to convict people who have committed crimes. *Private detectives*, also called *private investigators*, investigate crimes and provide security services for businesses and individuals. They are employed by private companies, but often cooperate with government law enforcement officials.

Corrections officers may be employed by local, state, and federal governments. They guard people who have been arrested and are awaiting trial, as well as people who have been convicted of a crime. Corrections officers are often in contact with dangerous individuals and must be on the alert for disturbances and violence against themselves and other prisoners.

Parole is the conditional release of a prisoner from a correctional facility who has not served out a full sentence. A long-standing practice of the U.S. justice system, parole is granted for a variety of reasons, including the "good behavior" of a prisoner, as well as overcrowding in prisons. Prisoners on parole, or parolees, are assigned to a *parole officer* upon their release. It is the job of the parole officer to meet periodically with the parolee to ensure that the terms of the release are followed; to provide guidance and counseling; and to help the parolee find a job,

housing, a therapist, or any other means of support. Parolees who break the release agreement may be returned to prison. A job with similar responsibilities is that of *probation officer*, and some officers handle both parolees and those on probation. As the title suggests, probation officers work with offenders who are given probation, which is the conditional suspension of a prison sentence immediately after conviction.

Crime analysts analyze patterns in criminal behavior—attempting to predict patterns and to discern criminals' motives—in order to catch criminals and to improve law enforcement response times. *Crime scene evidence technicians* collect and photograph relevant evidence, such as fingerprints, hairs, and bullets, at a crime scene. *Criminalists* scientifically analyze, compare, and evaluate physical evidence in the laboratory. They may perform autopsies to determine the cause of a person's death, or analyze fingerprints, hair, fibers, blood, and other evidence discovered at a crime scene. *Criminologists* study and research crime from a sociological perspective. They usually work in a university setting rather than for a law enforcement agency. *Forensic psychologists* use criminal evidence or behavior patterns to make a psychological analysis of a criminal and his or her motivations.

Polygraph examiners administer lie detection tests for local, state, and government agencies, as well as for private businesses. They are specially trained in operating polygraph equipment and in interpreting the results.

Deputy U.S. marshals report to the U.S. attorney general as part of the Department of Justice. Their responsibilities include providing security for the courts, including the judges and other officials, jurors, and witnesses. They also serve warrants and process documents, locate and arrest fugitives, transport prisoners, and manage the Federal Witness Security Program.

FBI special agents investigate violations of more than 200 federal laws and operate intelligence activities relating to domestic security matters. Employees of the FBI also work in the Bureau's laboratory in Washington, D.C., and maintain the world's largest fingerprint identification program. Special agents are also employed by the Secret Service and other branches of federal law enforcement.

Intelligence officers are federal employees who gather, analyze, and report information about the activities of domestic and international groups, and governments of foreign countries, in order to protect the interests and security of the United States. Intelligence officers may be either *case officers,* who work in the field and most often overseas; or *analysts,* who examine information, and who are generally located in offices in and around Washington, D.C. Intelligence officers work for the Central Intelligence Agency, the National Security Agency, the Department of Homeland Security, as well as for each branch of the armed forces. Intelligence officers and FBI special agents must meet particularly rigid educational, physical, and emotional requirements.

Cryptographic technicians are employed by government intelligence agencies, but also by private businesses such as banks. They specialize in coding and decoding messages, documents, and other communications so that their contents remain secret.

Customs officials and *border patrol agents* are employed by the Department of Homeland Security. Customs officials perform a wide variety of duties including preventing terrorists and terrorist weapons from entering the United States, controlling imports and exports, and combating smuggling and revenue fraud. *Border patrol agents* patrol the borders the United States shares with Canada and Mexico to ensure that people do not enter the country illegally, prevent the smuggling of illegal drugs, and ensure that individuals identified as terrorists do not enter the United States.

Airport security personnel is a blanket term describing all workers who protect the safety of passengers and staff in the nation's airports and aircraft. One of the largest group of personnel in this line of work is *security screeners,* who are responsible for identifying dangerous objects or hazardous materials in baggage, in cargo, or on traveling passengers, and for preventing these objects and their carriers from boarding planes. Also included in this group of workers are *air marshals,* who act as on-board, undercover security agents, protecting passengers, pilots, and other airline staff in the case of any emergencies while in the air.

Firefighters are generally employees of local governments. They protect peo-

Federal Prison Stats

In August 2005, more than 169,000 people were incarcerated in federal prisons. The following chart details their offenses.

Type of Offense	Number Incarcerated	Percentage
Drug Offenses	90,635	53.4
Weapons, Explosives, Arson	22,628	13.3
Immigration	19,065	11.2
Robbery	10,067	5.9
Extortion, Fraud, Bribery	6,993	4.1
Burglary, Larceny, Property Offenses	6,870	4.1
Homicide, Aggravated Assault, and Kidnapping Offenses	5,393	3.2
Miscellaneous	3,784	2.2
Sex Offenses	1,806	1.1
Banking and Insurance, Counterfeit, Embezzlement	925	0.5
Courts or Corrections	721	0.4
Continuing Criminal Enterprise	601	0.4
National Security	108	0.1

Source: Federal Bureau of Prisons

ple and property from fires and other emergencies by fighting fires, rescuing people trapped or injured by fires or other accidents. They also provide education on fire safety. Firefighters are in constant danger of injury; they must be courageous, physically strong, and able to work as part of a carefully coordinated team.

Fire inspectors perform examinations to enforce fire-prevention laws, ordinances, and codes; promote the development and use of effective fire-prevention methods; and provide instruction to the fire department and the general public regarding fire codes and prevention. *Fire investigators* analyze the cause, origin, and circumstances of fires involving loss of life and considerable property damage; interrogate witnesses and prepare investigation reports; and arrest and seek prosecution of arsonists.

Emergency medical technicians (EMTs) give immediate first aid treatment to sick or injured persons both at the scene and en route to the hospital or other medical facility. Many EMTs work for private ambulance services. Others are in municipal fire, police, or rescue departments, and a small percentage work in hospitals and medical centers. Also, there are many who volunteer, particularly in more rural areas, where there often are no paid EMTs at all.

Wildland firefighters work to combat the massive fires that occur in forests. If the blaze covers a large area, local departments can be called in to assist firefighters who work for the U.S. Forest Service and are stationed in the nation's forests. These firefighters locate fires from remote fire-lookout stations and report their findings to headquarters by telephone or radio. *Fire rangers* also patrol areas of the forest to find and report fires and hazardous conditions, as well as to ensure that travelers and campers comply with fire regulations. When fires break out, an elite corps of firefighters, known as *smoke-jumpers*, battle the blaze by parachuting from airplanes to reach inaccessible areas. Helicopters outfitted with large buckets (carrying between 72 and 2,600 gallons) dump huge amounts of water on burning areas.

Private security services are provided by *security consultants*, *security guards*, and *bodyguards*. Generally, these people work as part of companies providing security services to a range of businesses, individuals, and public and private facilities. Security consultants help businesses establish systems to protect their property, employees, and information. Security systems often include security guards, who are stationed at both public and private buildings and facilities. Bodyguards provide individual protection services for executives, politicians, celebrities, and others who desire privacy and safety.

Secret Service special agents employed by the Secret Service provide protection for politicians and political candidates—especially the president of the United States—and their families. In addition to protection duties, Secret Service agents also participate in criminal investigations involving law enforcement, administration, intelligence, forensics, security, information technology, communications, and other specialized areas.

Emergency and protective service careers offer opportunities to serve your community and to help others. Usually, these jobs also offer wide-ranging responsibilities, excitement, opportunities for advancement, and some exposure to dangerous situations. No matter what your personality type or temperament, there are careers in this field that will suit you.

EMPLOYMENT OPPORTUNITIES

As you've probably already figured out, employment opportunities in this field are quite diverse. You could work for a local agency or department, a state organization, or a federal agency like the FBI or the U.S. Department of Homeland Security. (See the "Structure of the Industry" section of this chapter for a rundown

The Truth about Polygraphs

During the 1920s and 1930s, it was discovered that certain physical processes, such as heart rate, breathing rate, and perspiration rate, responded to stress and could therefore be used to detect whether a person was lying. Special machines, called *polygraphs* or *lie detectors*, were constructed that could measure these processes while a suspected criminal was being questioned. Polygraphs can also be used to screen out unreliable people from sensitive positions and have been adopted by many private companies and government agencies when hiring new employees.

of some of the local, state, federal, and private agencies and companies.)

Most careers in emergency and protective services have clear-cut entry requirements. These range from requirements for a high school diploma for police officers, to bachelor's and even advanced degrees for special agents and intelligence officers. Certain law enforcement positions require highly specialized scientific knowledge. Some employers also require several years of related work experience, while others (such as the FBI) dictate a specific age range for hiring. The application process for some of these jobs is notoriously thorough and time consuming, but don't be discour-

aged by the paperwork. If you're the kind of person who has a strong sense of responsibility and a commitment to ensuring the well-being of others, you're halfway there.

INDUSTRY OUTLOOK

Employment opportunities in emergency and protective services careers should be good during the next decade. Public anxiety over crime and terrorism have led to demands for heightened law enforcement efforts, tougher sentencing laws, and dramatic increases in the security services industry. Since 1995, several incidents have raised concern over domestic security, particularly the threat of terrorist attacks. The bombing at the Alfred P. Murrah Federal Building in Oklahoma City in 1995, and the attacks on the World Trade Center in New York City and the Pentagon in Washington, D.C., in 2001 have caused an increase in both domestic and foreign intelligence and investigative operations. The threat of terrorism has put all public safety officials on alert, from FBI and CIA experts to local police forces and private security companies. There is now increased security throughout the country, particularly in and around government offices, public buildings, airports, post offices, financial centers, and media headquarters.

The "war on drugs" begun during the 1980s created a need for larger numbers of law enforcement officials trained and dedicated to reducing levels of drug trafficking. In the mid-1990s, President Clinton passed new tough-on-crime legislation that increased the numbers of police officers employed at the local, state, and federal levels. This focus on eradicating illegal drugs and their suppliers continues today, and police and other professionals will be needed to continue the fight.

The corrections industry has recorded an increase of more than 35 percent in the number of prisoners since the end of 1994, according to the U.S. Department of Justice. The war on drugs has had an especially great impact on the numbers of people being sent to prison. Public outrage at the early release of many violent criminals has led to demands for legislation to ensure that these criminals serve the full length of their sentences. More prisons are being built to accommodate them, and more corrections officers are being hired to guard them. At the same time, the overcrowding of many correctional facilities has stimulated pressure for more liberal probation and parole efforts, requiring greater numbers of parole and probation officers.

Immigration and customs officials have seen huge increases in the numbers of people and goods, especially drugs, entering the country illegally. Illegal immigration has become an area of national concern as more and more people have entered the country without the required visas and work permits. Crackdowns on illegal immigration have led to increased numbers of border patrol officers and immigration officials not only to patrol the country's borders, but also to seek out illegal immigrants in communities across the United States. Again, the threat of terrorism has had

an effect: border patrol personnel identify and apprehend suspected terrorists and others who might have criminal intent in addition to guarding for illegal entry.

Intelligence activities remain an important element of government, despite the end of the Cold War. The breakup of the Soviet Union has created new political situations and instabilities that must be continually monitored and analyzed for their effect on the interests and security of the United States. There is a continued risk of terrorist attacks in the United States and on U.S. targets overseas, and a primary function of the country's intelligence agencies is to identify, intercept, and pursue terrorists who seek to harm the country, its citizens, and its allies.

Private security activities have been stepped up, especially as many U.S. companies have begun to compete in a global economy. An especially fast-growing area of corporate security is in computer technology, as computers and computer transmissions of information have become more commonplace in most industries.

Employment of firefighters will grow faster than the average through 2014, according to the U.S. Department of Labor. Because they perform such a vital function in ensuring public safety, it's unlikely that their numbers will decrease at any point in the foreseeable future. In addition, as smaller communities grow, they will probably organize their own permanent fire departments. Employment for emergency medical technicians is expected to grow much faster than the average through 2014, according to the U.S. Department of Labor. Currently, the demand for these professionals exceeds the number of people who are trained to do the work. As the general population grows and the baby boomer generation ages., the need for more medical personnel is increasing, particularly in larger metropolitan communities.

SECTION 2

Careers

Border Patrol Agents

SUMMARY

Definition
Border patrol agents patrol more than 8,000 miles of U.S. border and are responsible for detecting and preventing smuggling and the illegal entry of aliens into the United States.

Alternative Job Titles
Border patrol officers

Salary Range
$24,000 to $37,000 to $58,000+

Educational Requirements
High school diploma

Certification or Training
Border patrol training academy

Employment Outlook
Faster than the average

High School Subjects
Foreign language (Spanish)
Geography
Government
Law
Physical education

Personal Interests
Camping/hiking
Exercise/personal fitness
Helping people: protection
Law
Student government

The sky is inky black, with only a sliver of moon casting a faint glow on Clara Reed Torres as she walks alongside the Rio Grande River. She crouches down now and again to take a closer look at the ground, then scans the Mexican side of the river for activity. The agents who just finished their shift had reported suspicious activity in the area, so Clara and her partner are checking for any signs of illegal immigrants, drug trafficking, or other illegal activities.

Out of the corner of her eye, she notices the leaves of a nearby shrub flutter in the windless night. She pushes aside a branch and sees the scuffed shoes first, then shines her flashlight beam into the nervous eyes of a Mexican man. Clara asks the man a few questions in Spanish, looks at the obviously forged identification card, and arrests the man. Later, a background check at the station will confirm that the man made his way illegally across the border into Texas. But by that time Clara is back in the field, checking more miles of river.

WHAT DOES A BORDER PATROL AGENT DO?

In many cases when someone from another country wants to work, study, or vacation in the United States, he or he has to apply for a special visa to do so. And if that person wishes to move here permanently, he or she must apply for citizenship. However, many people attempt to cross the U.S. border without a visa—and that's where border patrol agents enter the picture.

Border patrol agents are hired by Customs and Border Protection of the U.S. Department of Homeland Security to serve as the nation's gatekeepers. One of the agents' major activities is patrolling the border to prevent the illegal entry of aliens and arresting or deporting those who attempt to enter illegally. There are agents stationed at every border entry point in the United States, but most heavily along the Mexican border in Arizona, California, New Mexico, and Texas. At these regular crossings, border patrol agents check all cars for people or items hidden in the vehicle. Deciding which cars to stop is almost an art form for border patrol agents. A car that is moving erratically or riding low to the ground could be a sign that it is loaded down with people. Border patrol agents also become experts at spotting a false identification card almost instantly or discerning a tourist from an illegal alien by asking a single question. Agents are authorized to arrest and take into custody illegal aliens or people they suspect of smuggling.

But most illegal aliens don't attempt to cross into the United States at the official borders. Instead, they wait until nightfall and then try to cross in isolated areas where they hope to go undetected. That's why border patrol agents actually perform a great deal of their work in rugged and uninhabited mountains, canyons, deserts, and waterways. Border patrol agents have become known throughout the law enforcement community for their excellent tracking skills, language skills, wilderness survival skills, and their 24-hour availability. In certain areas, the agents even travel on horseback, by jeep, by mountain bike, and by helicopter, using special techniques and equipment such as electronic sensors, night-vision goggles, and other covert surveillance devices.

Border patrol agents also canvas known pickup and drop-off points for illegal aliens and smugglers. For instance, they might check a small town's convenience store, where a phone booth has been used previously for calls to a professional smuggler. Or they might check out an area where piles of clothing and food supplies have been found.

Another part of their work involves assisting different federal and local law enforcement agencies in stopping the flow of drugs and other contraband from being smuggled into the United States, as well as in preventing terrorists and terrorist weapons from entering the country. In recent years, the increase in drug traffic from Central and South America has had a major impact on the duties of border patrol agents. Currently, the prevention of drug smuggling is a large part of the job—and a dangerous part as well. Armed encounters

Lingo to Learn

coyote Slang term for an alien smuggler.

jeep-plane team Teams that coordinate aerial surveillance with ground operations, so that wide expanses of border can be covered.

linewatch A routine activity in which agents patrol the border for would-be crossers and apprehend them.

muster room A large room where border patrol agents gather to get information and assignments at the beginning of a shift.

OTM This acronym stand for "Other Than Mexican." Aliens are classified as Mexican or OTM.

sign cutting A technique in which agents smooth the surface of sandy areas along areas used for illegal entries. When these sand traps are examined, they show footprints. Agents can follow the "signs" and apprehend the offenders.

stillwatch An agent sits and watches a specific area in order to deter any would-be crossers.

between professional smugglers and border patrol agents have increased markedly, especially in certain sectors of the Mexico–United States border. Because of the risks involved, all agents are specially trained in the use of weaponry. At some border crossings in Arizona and Southern California where agents have been shot at, injured, and even killed by smugglers, the agents now wear bulletproof vests and carry automatic weapons.

WHAT IS IT LIKE TO BE A BORDER PATROL AGENT?

Clara Reed Torres has worked as a border patrol agent for 13 years. She is currently a supervisory border patrol agent at the Weslaco Border Patrol Station in Weslaco, Texas.

Border patrol agents at Clara's station work one of three shifts: 8:00 A.M. to 4:00 P.M., 4:00 P.M. to 12:00 A.M., or 12:00 A.M. to 8:00 A.M. Clara currently works the 8:00 A.M. to 4:00 P.M. shift. On a typical shift, Clara meets in the "muster room" with agents who are coming on duty, as well as those whose shift is ending. The off-going agents provide information on special problems or alien foot traffic patterns that have occurred. This is also the time when agents are given their location assignments for the shift. When all that business is done, the agents "break muster" and head out to their patrol areas.

As a supervisory border patrol agent, Clara has both administrative and patrol duties. Her administrative duties involve assisting in the processing of illegal immigrants who have been apprehended, completing paperwork and other reports, and supervising staff. Her patrol duties require her to monitor large sections of the Rio Grande River, which creates a natural border between the United States and Mexico. Once she arrives at her post, she walks up and down the river, watching for any movement or unusual activity. "Our main focus as agents," she explains, "is stopping illegal immigration. We are at the river to apprehend people who are illegally in the United States. Our presence also deters those people who are across the border in Mexico who want to enter the country illegally. In addition, Customs and Border Protection is part of the U.S. Department of Homeland Security, so in the process of securing our borders against illegal immigration, we also have a goal of detecting any possible sign of terrorism-related activities." Agents also focus on the illegal smuggling of narcotics. "Unfortunately," Clara says, "the drug trade is a big problem. I've encountered everything from marijuana to heroin to methamphetamines to steroids."

During her shift, Clara may arrest a number of illegal aliens, or the border area she's covering may be quiet. "Today," she explains, "I may apprehend 72 people at the river, tomorrow I may get nothing, the next day I may apprehend hundreds of people." When Clara apprehends an individual, she questions the person to determine his or her citizenship and immigration status, and then, if the individual is proven to be an illegal immigrant, she reads the individual his or her rights. After that, she calls for a transport unit to pick up the person and take him or her to the station for processing, which involves creating a file that contains biographical data, as well as fingerprinting the individual. "After we take their fingerprints," Clara says, "we run a criminal check to see if the person has been deported before or is wanted for other crimes."

Clara considers shift work to be the only downfall of the job. "You have no energy after working three weeks on a night shift," she says. "You may sleep seven hours a day, but it's not the same as sleeping at night." Overall, though, Clara loves her job. "I am very proud to wear the uniform," she says. "You get a lot of public recognition. People notice you and thank you for protecting the borders."

DO I HAVE WHAT IT TAKES TO BE A BORDER PATROL AGENT?

Being a border patrol agent requires a unique blend of qualities that include assertiveness, the ability to work under stress, and quick decision-making skills. An agent must be able to analyze a situation on the spot and to calmly defuse a volatile moment.

To Be a Successful Border Patrol Agent, You Should . . .

- be tough, yet compassionate, when apprehending illegal aliens
- be able to work under stress and in physically demanding environments
- have a strong sense of direction and experience with the geography of wilderness areas
- be well organized and motivated
- be able to communicate effectively in writing, since there is a certain amount of paperwork and report writing involved
- be able to speak fluent Spanish

An agent also needs to be compassionate. Many people who attempt to enter the United States illegally have undergone extreme risk and hardship, and border patrol agents just as frequently encounter emotionally moving situations as hostile, violent ones. Agents must be able to work at enforcing what, at times, may seem a futile and frustrating task. "Compassion is a big part of the job," says Clara. "You have to be able to use your discretion to know what to do with each specific individual. I would say that 90 percent of the people who we apprehend are in the United States to just make a better living. Compassion is key because you come across a lot of people who are in distress who we end up rescuing rather than simply apprehending. The other 10 percent are the more aggressive criminals, drug smugglers, alien smugglers, and terrorism suspects."

Border patrol agents also "really need to have a good sense of direction, and if you don't, you really need to learn your area," says Clara. "The areas that we patrol are so big. They don't consist of five different streets or 10 different neighborhoods; they stretch far along the Rio Grande River. Farms, ranches, brush areas . . . they all look alike, so you really need to know your surroundings." Because they work long shifts in sometimes harsh terrain, it's also absolutely vital that border patrol agents have physical stamina and strength.

Because they often work with little supervision, border patrol agents should be able to plan and organize their own work schedule. They should be able to communicate effectively in writing, since there is a certain amount of paperwork and report writing involved.

HOW DO I BECOME A BORDER PATROL AGENT?
Education
High School

The minimum educational requirement for anyone wishing to train as a border patrol agent is a high school diploma, although an associate's degree is preferred. If you are still in high school, take geography, social studies, and government courses. This will help give you a general background for the field. Take a foreign language class, specifically, Spanish; fluency in this language will give you an advantage over other job applicants. A solid understanding of the basic rules of English will also help, since good communication skills are crucial to pass the written entrance exam, as well as once you're in the training academy and on the job.

Postsecondary Training

For the high school graduate with a strong interest in becoming a border patrol agent, an associate's degree or three years of work experience is recommended. And again, studying Spanish could give candidates a solid head start, since the amount of language taught during the training academy is equivalent to two years of college-level Spanish.

On-the-Job Training

Everyone hired as a border patrol agent has to complete a 19-week training academy in Artesia, New Mexico. At the academy, trainees receive intensive instruction in Spanish, immigration and nationality law, firearms, judo and physical training, arrest methods, methods of tracking and surveillance, self-defense, court procedures, as well as report writing, fingerprinting, care and use of firearms, and pursuit driving. Clara notes that border patrol agents have to become extremely knowledgeable in immigration law. "The average trainee spends two to three hours each day just studying law," she says.

After graduation, the trainee reports to his or her duty station and attends a post-academy class once a week. This training focuses on law instruction and Spanish language. During the first 10 months of employment, the trainee's progress is graded two times. He or she must pass a Spanish exam and law exam after 6 months on the job, and the final test is given after 10 months.

Internships and Volunteerships

Because of the nature of border patrol work, you will not be able to receive direct internship or volunteer experience with Customs and Border Protection. If you attend a postsecondary program in criminal justice or a related field, you will have the opportunity to participate in an internship with a law enforcement organization. You might also consider volunteering with your local police department to get an idea of the responsibilities and duties of law enforcement professionals.

Advancement Possibilities

Senior patrol agents are experienced agents who train and oversee new border patrol agents.

Border patrol supervisors oversee the staff of a border patrol station. Depending on the size of their facility, they may also have patrol duties.

Customs and Border Protection agents monitor more than 300 ports of entry to the United States.

Labor Unions

Border patrol agents may become members of the National Border Patrol Council. The union is recommended but not required. It protects agents against unfair labor practices and disciplinary actions, and also works to improve working conditions and salaries.

WHO WILL HIRE ME?

There's no question of who your employer will be if you enter this field. All border patrol agents are employees of the Department of Homeland Security's Customs and Border Protection (CBP). The CBP accepts applications during a certain period of time known as an "open period." You can write or call the CBP to find out when this period is and to get an application (see information in the "Look to the Pros" chapter of Section 4: What Can I Do Right Now?), or get additional details at the CBP's Web site (http://www.cbp.gov). Basic qualifications for consideration by the Border Patrol include the following: you must be a U.S. citizen between the ages of 21 and 37, have a valid driver's license, and not have a criminal record.

The first step in applying for the Border Patrol involves taking a written U.S. Office of Personnel Management entrance exam. Those who earn high test scores go on a list of eligible applicants who are granted interviews. If the interview goes well, candidates take a medical exam, which includes a drug test and a physical fitness test, and have a background check. The entire process described above can take a matter of months. However, there is also an expedited hiring process for those willing to travel to certain testing and interview sites at their own expense. Ask about it when you contact CBP.

If you are selected and hired (on a probationary basis), the next step is the 19-week training academy described earlier in this chapter. After training, new border patrol agents are initially assigned to southern border stations. These assignments are made according to the needs at each sector, and new agents are not given a choice of their first duty station. Later in your career, you can request particular stations, although transfers to the northern stations along the United States–Canada border are rare and hard to get.

WHERE CAN I GO FROM HERE?

Overall, there are good prospects for advancement as a border patrol agent. After their first year, all border patrol agents advance to the GS-9 journeyman level. From there, a year later they advance to the GS-11 level. With experience and training, border patrol agents can advance to other positions with Customs and Border Protection, becoming a Customs and Border Protection agent, import specialist, or agriculture specialist, for instance.

There are also opportunities with other law enforcement agencies. These might include the U.S. Marshals, the Federal Bureau of Investigation, and the Drug Enforcement Agency.

Clara is eligible to retire at the age of 47 with 25 years of service, but she has not made a firm decision about whether she will take advantage of this opportunity. "I do plan to eventually complete my bachelor's degree and teach law enforcement at the college level," she says.

WHAT ARE THE SALARY RANGES?

Border patrol agents begin at either the GS-5 or GS-7 grade, depending on their level of education. In 2005 these grades paid $24,677 to $32,084 and $30,567 to $39,738 per year, respectively. GS-9 or journeyman salaries paid $37,390 to $48,604 per year. The highest nonsupervisory grade for a border patrol agent is GS-11, which paid between $45,239 and

$58,811 in 2005. Agents in certain cities, such as New York, Los Angeles, Boston, San Francisco, Chicago, and Washington, D.C., are entitled to receive additional locality pay, which adds roughly 16 percent to the base salary. Overtime and pay differentials for night, weekend, and holiday work can also greatly increase an agent's salary.

Because these are federal jobs, the salaries are generally higher than comparable law enforcement jobs with city, county, or state agencies. Other benefits include sick time and vacation time (the accrual rate for vacation time increases with years of service). Any injuries incurred on the job are covered by a government plan. There is also a choice of health plans for border patrol agents, depending upon where they are stationed. Agents can save for retirement under the Federal Employee Retirement System and may also enroll in the Thrift Savings Plan.

WHAT IS THE JOB OUTLOOK?

From Clara's perspectives, employment prospects for border patrol agents are good, but she says that aspiring agents "must be willing to relocate and take on shift work."

Employment opportunities for border patrol agents have grown significantly over the past decade. This growth can largely be attributed to the United States government's expanded effort to curb the increase in smuggling and illegal immigration along the Mexico border, as well as its renewed efforts to thwart terrorists from entering the United States after the terrorist attacks of September 11, 2001. More job openings can be anticipated in the future as well, thanks to better public awareness about illegal immigration and ongoing government-backed efforts to crack down on drug smuggling and to deter terrorism.

Related Jobs

- air marshals
- bailiffs
- corrections officers
- deputy sheriffs
- deputy U.S. marshals
- detectives
- drug enforcement agents
- FBI agents
- fish and game wardens
- intelligence officers
- internal affairs investigators
- military police officers
- narcotics investigators
- park rangers
- police officers
- private investigators
- Secret Service special agents
- security screeners
- state highway patrol officers

It is important to note, however, that these are regarded as desirable federal jobs, and because of rigorous hiring standards, the competition is always stiff. After the initial probationary period, the job security for a border patrol agent is good. There is very low turnover in the field, especially compared to other law enforcement positions.

Corrections Officers

SUMMARY

Definition
Corrections officers guard people who have been arrested and are awaiting trial or who have been tried, convicted, and sentenced to serve time in a penal institution.

Alternative Job Titles
Correctional officers
Detentions officers
Jailers

Salary Range
$22,000 to $33,000 to $54,000+

Educational Requirements
High school diploma

Certification or Licensing
Required by certain states

Employment Outlook
More slowly than the average

High School Subjects
Government
Physical education
Psychology
Sociology

Personal Interests
Exercise/personal fitness
Helping people: protection
Law
Sports
Student government

Checking prisoners in and out as they enter the general population or are taken to court, serving inmates lunch, inspecting inmates' rooms for cleanliness and contraband, observing the inmate population for potential signs of trouble. "It all sounds pretty simple," says Anthony Listy, a corrections officer in New Mexico, "until you realize that these are the same people who cannot follow the laws of our society. I may deal with anywhere from 30 to 130 different personalities that are coming off of alcohol or drugs; they are angry, scared, stressed out, or have psychiatric problems. This is where you really began to understand what it means to be a corrections officer. You are not just someone who goes around opening and closing doors; you are a combination of police officer, counselor, emergency medical first responder, referee, teacher, interpreter, social worker, and many other roles that we take on as leader of the unit."

WHAT DOES A CORRECTIONS OFFICER DO?

Corrections officers are hired by federal, state, and local prisons and jails to maintain order according to the institution's policies, regulations, and procedures. They are concerned with the safekeeping of people who have been arrested and are awaiting trial or who have been tried and found guilty, and are serving time in a correctional institution.

Corrections officers keep watch over inmates around the clock—while they're eating, sleeping, exercising, bathing, and working. In order to prevent disturbances, corrections officers carefully observe the conduct and behavior of inmates. They watch for forbidden activities, as well as for poor adjustment to prison life. They try to settle disputes before violence can erupt. They may search the inmates or their living quarters for weapons or drugs and inspect locks, bars on windows and doors, and gates for any sign of tampering. They conduct regular head counts to make sure all inmates are accounted for. Some corrections officers are stationed on towers and at gates to prevent escapes. In the case of a major disturbance, a corrections officer may have to use a weapon or force. After such a violation or disturbance, corrections officers are responsible for filing detailed reports. Corrections officers cannot show favoritism and must report any inmate who breaks the rules.

Corrections officers assign work projects to the inmates, supervise them while they carry out their work, and teach them about unfamiliar tasks. Officers try to ensure inmates' health and safety by checking the cells for unsanitary conditions and fire hazards. They are in charge of screening visitors at the entrance and inspecting mail for prohibited items. Officers are also responsible for escorting inmates from one area of the prison to another and helping them get medical

assistance. Certain officers are charged with transporting inmates between courthouses, prisons, mental institutions, or other destinations.

Some officers specialize in guarding juvenile offenders who are being held at a police station or detention house pending a hearing. These officers often investigate the background of first offenders to check for a criminal history and to make a recommendation to the court. Lost or runaway children are also placed in the custody of these officers until their parents or guardians can be contacted. In small communities, corrections officers may also serve as deputy sheriffs or police officers.

The person in charge of supervising other corrections officers is often called the *head corrections officer*. This person assigns duties, directs the activities of groups of inmates, arranges for the release and transfer of inmates, and maintains overall security measures.

While psychologists and social workers work at the prison to counsel inmates, a secondary aspect of a corrections officer's job is to provide informal counseling. Officers may talk with inmates in order to help them adjust to prison life, prepare for return to civilian life, and avoid committing crimes in the future. On a more immediate level, they can help inmates arrange a visit to the library, get in touch with their families, suggest how to look for a job after being released from prison, or discuss personal problems. Corrections officers who have college degrees in psychology or criminology often take on these more rehabilitative responsibilities.

Lingo to Learn

contraband Any forbidden item that is in a prisoner's possession.

house An inmate will refer to his cell as his "house."

run A hallway lined with inmates' cells.

shakedown Corrections officers conduct a thorough search of an inmate's cell, looking for contraband.

yard-out This means that it's time for the inmates to go to the yard for exercise. Correctional officers also say "chow-out" when it's time for the inmates to eat and "shower-out" when it's time for showers.

Corrections officers keep a daily record of their activities and make regular reports to their supervisors. These reports concern the behavior of the inmates, the quality and quantity of work they do, as well as any disturbances, rule violations, and unusual occurrences. Because prison security has to be maintained at all times, corrections officers sometimes are expected to work nights, weekends, and holidays. Generally, a workweek consists of five eight-hour days. Work takes place both indoors and outdoors, depending on the officer's assigned duties on a given day. Conditions range from a well-lit, well-ventilated area to a hot, noisy, and overcrowded one.

WHAT IS IT LIKE TO BE A CORRECTIONS OFFICER?

Anthony Listy is a corrections officer for the Bernalillo County Metropolitan Deten-

tion Center—the largest county correctional facility in the state of New Mexico, housing more than 2,300 inmates. Anthony has been a corrections officer since 1983. He says that he originally took the job as a stepping-stone into a government job. "I had no idea what a corrections officer was or what one did," he recalls. "I found that it was something I could do, and each day was a challenge. Unlike many jobs, every day is different when you are dealing with inmates. It keeps you alert, and you learn on a daily basis."

Corrections officers at Anthony's facility work an eight-hour shift for a total of 40 hours a week. There are three shifts per 24-hour period: Day, 7:00 A.M. to 3:00 P.M.; Swing, 3:00 P.M. to 11:00 P.M.; and Graveyard, 11:00 P.M. to 7:00 A.M. "We have plenty of overtime," he says. "It is not unusual to work two or three double shifts (16 hours) in a week. Overtime can run from two to eight hours."

Anthony begins his workday by attending a briefing before his shift begins. There, he and the other corrections officers going on duty find out everything that's happened and learn which area they'll be working that day. This area can vary from day to day. "One day," he explains, "I may be with the hard-core population inmates and the next day in the booking area." For the most part, Anthony works in the intake area. "This is where inmates who cannot make bond are brought to make the transition into [the prison] population," he explains. Anthony takes a headcount of the inmates—verifying the number of and identification of inmates in his assigned area. "Once I've completed this, I prepare a list of all inmates going to court from my area, get them up, and have them prepare for court," he says. "They will be required to make their beds, clean their rooms, and shower prior to being interviewed by court personnel. They are then lined up and readied for transport to court. Once my 'courts' have departed I inspect the inmates' rooms for cleanliness and search for contraband. Any violations are handled as per policy. After this, I begin preparing the remaining inmates to be classified. A classification specialist then interviews the inmates who need to be classified."

Over the next several hours, Anthony prepares any additional court lists that he receives, serves the inmates lunch, and observes them in order to maintain order. After these tasks are completed, Anthony receives a list from the classification specialist that details the inmates who have been interviewed and where to move them. "I move all appropriate inmates and update the computer to reflect these moves," he explains. "By this time the inmates taken to court start returning, new inmates are arriving from the booking area, and a few are taken to releasing to be kicked out. By then it is time to lock the unit down and prepare for headcount—once again verifying the number and identification of all inmates on the unit."

In addition to monitoring and facilitating the movement of inmates, Anthony must keep a log throughout his entire shift. "The log is a chronological report of

To Be a Successful Corrections Officer, You Should . . .

- not be easily intimidated or influenced by the inmates
- have physical and emotional strength to handle sometimes violent or abusive prisoners
- be able to use persuasion rather than brute force to get inmates to follow the rules
- be able to stay alert and aware of prisoners' actions and attitudes
- have sound judgment and the ability to think and act quickly
- be able to communicate clearly both verbally and in writing

everything that has taken place and everyone who has entered and/or departed from the unit," he explains. "There are a number of reports that need to be generated, such as a razor log [that tracks personal razors that are given to inmates so that they can shave every other day], inspection sheets, and so on. When the next shift arrives to relieve me, I brief them on the count, on any unfinished work that needs to be completed, and, most importantly, on how the inmates were behaving (especially if there is a particular inmate to keep an eye on)."

Anthony may also be assigned to work in several other posts such as *classification specialist*, *disciplinary chairman*, *ID officer*, and *releasing officer*. "We currently have a system of separating inmates by such things as charges, history (penitentiary time), age, gang affiliation, and attitude," Anthony explains. "This is all done by the classification specialist, who interviews the inmate and does background checks. The disciplinary chairman decides what type of discipline an inmate will receive when he violates one of the facility's rules. ID officers are responsible for fingerprinting and making a positive identification while the inmate is being booked. The releasing officer is responsible for reviewing all the documentation for the release of an inmate and making sure that the correct inmate gets released."

DO I HAVE WHAT IT TAKES TO BE A CORRECTIONS OFFICER?

There's no denying that handling the inherent stress of this line of work takes a unique person. In a maximum-security facility, the environment is often noisy, crowded, poorly ventilated, and even dangerous. Corrections officers need the physical and emotional strength to handle the stress involved in working with criminals, some of whom may be violent. "There is the potential for extreme danger," says Chuck Gallego, a corrections officer for nearly 17 years who is currently assigned to the Work Furlough–Work Release Unit in the Pima County (Arizona) Sheriff's Department. "We have had officers beaten badly and one taken hostage. You really have to use interpersonal communication skills in

this job. I personally have not been struck on purpose by an inmate, though I have been involved in taking control of inmates by myself on a few occasions." A corrections officer has to stay alert and aware of prisoners' actions and attitudes. This constant vigilance can be hard on some people. Work in a minimum-security prison is usually more comfortable, cleaner, and less stressful.

Officers need to use persuasion rather than brute force to get inmates to follow the rules. Certain inmates take a disproportionate amount of time and attention because they're either violent, mentally ill, or victims of abuse by other inmates. Officers have to carry out routine duties while being alert for the unpredictable outbursts. Sound judgment and the ability to think and act quickly are important qualities for corrections officers. With experience and training, corrections officers are usually able to handle volatile situations without resorting to physical force.

The ability to communicate clearly orally and in writing is extremely important. Corrections officers have to write a number of reports, documenting routine procedures as well as any violations by the inmates. "You have to have good writing skills (there are lots of reports), and good basic computer skills," Anthony Listy says. A correction officer's eight-hour shift can easily extend to ten hours because of the reports that must be written.

An effective corrections officer is not easily intimidated or influenced by the inmates. "You have to be firm and fair in your enforcement of the rules, and vigilant in the running of your housing

Pros and Cons of Being a Corrections Officer

The editors of *What Can I Do Now?: Safety & Security* asked corrections officer Anthony Listy what he felt were the pros and cons of work in this career.

PROS

- Good pay and retirement benefits, and good opportunities for fast advancement in rank.

- Many educational opportunities, mostly in law enforcement–related courses.

- This work will allow you to learn a lot about people and how to communicate with them. We deal with people at their worst, which is most challenging. Unlike police officers, judges, and prosecutors who deal with offenders only on a short-term basis, corrections officers are with them 8 to 16 hours a day, every day.

- If you plan on going into law enforcement, corrections is the best way to start because it will afford you a better understanding of the clientele you will be dealing with so you can work more effectively.

- Corrections is a hard, stressful job that can be very rewarding to those who have the courage to do it.

CONS

- Corrections is one of the most misunderstood and misjudged careers. We are not in the public eye like police and firefighters; therefore we do not share in their glamour. Kids always say that they want to be a police officer or firefighter, but not a corrections officer. In movies corrections officers are always portrayed as muscle-bound thugs who go around beating up poor prisoners. Corrections workers rarely receive the same respect even from the government that cops and firefighters enjoy.

- Corrections is not a job for just anybody; it's stressful, dangerous, and demanding, and it really does take someone special to come inside these walls, whether you are a corrections officer or support staff.

areas," advises Anthony. There's a misconception, however, that corrections officers need to be tough guys. While it's true that a person needs some physical strength to perform the job, corrections officers also need to be able to use their head to anticipate and defuse any potentially dangerous situations between inmates or between guards and inmates.

HOW DO I BECOME A CORRECTIONS OFFICER?
Education
High School

Entry requirements vary widely from state to state. A high school diploma, or its equivalent, is the minimum requirement for employment at most correctional institutions. While most high school classes are not directly relevant to corrections, health classes may offer an introduction to issues that will be covered thoroughly during formal training as a corrections officer, such as sanitation, universal precautions, and first aid.

English classes are recommended as well for anyone interested in a career as a corrections officer. At most prisons, jails, and penitentiaries, reports are required to be well written, with attention to sentence structure and spelling. Spanish would also be useful for future corrections officers who plan on working in a region of the country with a large Spanish-speaking population.

Postsecondary Training

Some correctional institutions require that corrections officers possess a college degree. In certain states, officers need two years of college with an emphasis on criminal justice or behavioral science, or three years as a correctional, military police, or licensed peace officer. Generally, states that require more education offer higher entry-level salaries and have shorter-duration training academies. At federal institutions, applicants must have at least two years of college or two years of work or military experience.

The most relevant areas of study in college include psychology, criminal justice, police science, and criminology. Some correctional facilities offer internships to students who are earning their degrees in these areas.

"I only had a basic high school education when I started," Anthony Listy says. "However, I have been able to further my education by taking courses related to law, law enforcement, and management. I have taken specialized training in dealing with psychiatric inmates, as well as CERT [Correctional Emergency Response Team] training (it's the corrections version of a SWAT team). Training is an ongoing thing in corrections. We train for medical emergencies. We train for fighting fires and evacuations due to fire and/or poisonous gases—we learn to use a lot of the same equipment as firefighters. We train to restrain and control violent inmates, and we learn self-defense. We train in riot control, fingerprinting, firearms, and many more areas related to our positions as corrections officers."

"I went to Pueblo High School on the south side of Tucson, Arizona, and that was educational training in itself," Chuck Gallego recalls. "I didn't take advantage of college courses. I went through a seven-week academy with the Arizona Department of Corrections and a seven-week academy with the Pima County Sheriff's Department Corrections Bureau that included a six-week Correctional Training Officer Program. I also utilized the supervisory skills I attained from my years of experience as a staff sergeant with the army."

Certification and Training

The American Correctional Association and the American Jail Association provide guidelines for prison training programs. These programs generally introduce new corrections officers to the policies of their particular institution and prepare them for handling work situations. The training lasts several weeks and includes crisis intervention, contraband control, counseling, self-defense, and use of firearms.

Training ranges from special academies to informal, on-the-job training. The Federal Bureau of Prisons operates its training center in Glynco, Georgia,

A Day in the Life of Chuck Gallego, Corrections Officer

The editors of *What Can I Do Now?: Safety & Security* asked corrections officer Chuck Gallego to describe a typical day on the job.

7:00 A.M.: I arrive for work and attend a briefing at the main jail.

7:25 A.M.: I arrive at my assigned post. I raise the flags (U.S. and Arizona flags), then get a handheld radio and a set of keys that can be used for most of the doors in the facility.

8:30 A.M.: The kitchen crew arrives (16 inmates). I must strip them out and give them clean jail uniforms to wear and send them to the housing area. I strip them out because they may be trying to introduce contraband into the facility.

9:00 A.M.: Work-furlough/work-release inmates begin to arrive from outside work; they are strip searched and sent to the housing area.

10:00 A.M.: I get a set of keys for a flatbed truck and take two inmates (known as Blues Brothers because some years ago they used to wear blue uniforms; they now wear red) with me to the supply dock and pick up big baskets that are approximately 4 feet high, 3.5 feet wide, and 4 feet long. They are full of uniforms, cleaning supplies, forms, blankets, and sheets. On Fridays, I also pick up soda and popcorn.

10:30 A.M.: More work-release inmates have returned and need to be strip searched.

11:00 A.M.: The supply crew has returned and needs to be stripped out.

11:30 A.M.: I ask a work crew of female inmates to stack the folded uniforms onto racks marked by uniform sizes and to clean the strip-out rooms and staff restrooms.

1:30 P.M.: The evening kitchen crew is ready to be pat searched and sent out while the morning kitchen crew is ready to be stripped out and sent back to the housing area. A total of 32 inmates are searched.

2:00 P.M.: More work-furlough/work-release inmates arrive to be stripped out and sent to the housing area.

2:30 P.M.: I try to squeeze in a soda and a snack (one of the officers here brings in food for all of the staff and has done so for years). We don't get a lunch, so we do the best that we can. (We are not allowed to leave the facility to eat.)

3:15 P.M.: The swing shift arrives after receiving a briefing. We brief them as to what is going on and what has happened throughout the day. I hand over my key and radio to the incoming escort officer and depart the building as my day has ended—provided that I don't get selected for overtime.

where new hires take part in a three-week training program.

Numerous certification programs are available to corrections officers; these are optional in most states. Common certifications include self-defense, weapons use, urinanalysis, shield and gun, shotgun/handgun, CPR, and cell extraction. Many officers also take advantage of additional training that is offered at their facility, such as suicide prevention, AIDS awareness, use of four-point restraints, and emergency preparedness. At most prisons, there is annual mandatory in-service training that focuses on policies and procedures. The American Correctional Association and the American Jail Association offer certification programs to corrections officers and corrections managers.

Internships and Volunteerships

Because of age requirements and the nature of the work, there are no opportunities for high school students to gain actual experience while still in school. Where the minimum age requirement is 21, prospective corrections officers may prepare for employment by taking college courses in criminal justice, psychology, police science, criminology, or a related field. If you pursue a two- or four-year degree, you will likely participate in an internship where you will assist experienced corrections officers as they go about their duties.

Labor Unions

Union membership is not required, but many correctional officers find it advantageous to join. Officers who work for state-run facilities can join the union for all state employees. In return for weekly or monthly dues, members receive services intended to improve their working conditions.

WHO WILL HIRE ME?

There are facilities in virtually every part of the country that need corrections officers. You could work in a prison or jail that houses men, women, juveniles, or a combination. Roughly 60 percent of officers work in state-run facilities. Many others are employed at city and county jails, while the smallest percentage works for the federal government. A number of officers are hired by privately run correctional facilities. Depending on where you live, you may also have the choice of maximum-, medium-, and minimum-security facilities.

To apply for a job, simply contact your state's department of corrections or the Federal Bureau of Prisons and request information about entrance requirements, training, and job opportunities. In addition, there are numerous journals that list job openings. For example, two of the professional organizations listed at the end of this book—the American Correctional Association and the Federal Bureau of Prisons—have both publications and Web sites with job listings. Another publication that posts job openings is the *Corrections Compendium* (http://www.aca.org/publications/ccjournal.asp).

Most correctional institutions require candidates to be at least 18 years old (sometimes 21 years old), have a high school diploma, and be a U.S. citizen with no criminal record. There are also health and physical strength requirements, and many states have minimum height, vision, and hearing standards. Other common requirements are a driver's license and a job record that shows you've been dependable.

WHERE CAN I GO FROM HERE?

Many officers take college courses in law enforcement or criminal justice to increase their chances of promotion. In some states, officers must serve two years in each position before they can be considered for a promotion.

With additional education and training, experienced officers can also be promoted to supervisory or administrative positions such as head corrections officer, assistant warden, or prison director. Officers who want to continue to work directly with offenders can move into various other positions. For example, *probation and parole officers* monitor and counsel offenders, process their release from prison, and evaluate their progress in becoming productive members of society. *Recreation leaders* organize and instruct offenders in sports, games, and arts and crafts.

Although Anthony Listy is eligible for retirement, he plans to work several more years, "at least," he says, "until I get a couple more of my kids into college." Chuck Gallego plans to retire in approximately four-and-a-half years and to work in a dif-

---

Advancement Possibilities

Head corrections officers supervise other corrections officers. They assign duties, direct the activities of inmates, arrange the release and transfer of inmates, and maintain overall security measures.

Wardens, sometimes known as *prison directors*, oversee all correctional staff. They are ultimately responsible for the safety of the prisoner population, as well as the security of the prison and its employees.

Probation and parole officers monitor and counsel offenders, process their release from prison, and evaluate their progress in becoming productive members of society.

---

ferent part of his county. "I might try to work as a deputy...although if I promote, I may stick around a bit longer."

WHAT ARE THE SALARY RANGES?

Wages for corrections officers vary considerably depending on their employers and their level of experience. According to the U.S. Department of Labor, the 2004 median annual earnings for corrections officers employed by the federal government were $44,540; for those employed by state governments, $36,870; and for those employed by local governments, $34,880. The U.S. Department of Labor reports that overall the lowest paid 10 percent of corrections officers earned less than $22,630 per year in 2004, and the highest paid 10 percent earned more than $54,820. Median earnings for corrections officers were $33,600.

The U.S. Department of Labor reports higher earnings for supervisors/managers, with a median yearly income of $44,720 in 2004. The lowest paid 10 percent earned less than $27,770, and the highest paid 10 percent earned more than $70,990.

Most corrections officers participate in medical and dental insurance plans offered by their facility, and can get disability and life insurance at group rates. They also receive vacation and sick leave, as well as retirement benefits. Many correctional facilities offer full retirement benefits for corrections officers after 20 years of service.

WHAT IS THE JOB OUTLOOK?

Corrections officers can count on steady employment and good job security. Prison security has to be maintained at all times, making corrections officers unlikely candidates for layoffs, even when there are budget cuts. These jobs are rarely affected by changes in the economy or government spending. Due to a high turnover rate, a budget can usually be trimmed by simply not replacing the officers who leave voluntarily.

"Unfortunately, corrections is a booming business," says Anthony Listy. "It's great for those of us in the profession because we have plenty of job security due to high crime rates. There are plenty of opportunities with both public and privately run facilities. Most facilities have excellent retirement plans and enough overtime to make it a worthwhile investment. You can work in this field and consider it as a stepping-stone into other law enforcement careers or stick with it to retirement. Even within the department, there are many opportunities for career changes."

There are other factors pointing to the strong job outlook for corrections officers. Prisons in the United States house at least 35 percent more prisoners than were incarcerated at the end of 1994, according

Related Jobs

- armored car guards
- bailiffs
- deputy sheriffs
- deputy U.S. marshals
- FBI agents
- immigration guards
- military police officers
- park rangers
- parole officers
- police officers
- probation officers
- Secret Service special agents
- security guards
- security screeners
- state highway patrol officers

to the U.S. Department of Justice, and new prisons are being built to house these inmates. This growth is expected to continue, with the trend in the United States being toward mandatory sentencing guidelines, longer sentences, and reduced parole. All of this translates into a strong need for more corrections officers. The U.S. Department of Labor predicts that the employment for corrections officers will grow more slowly than the average for all other occupations through 2014.

While entry-level jobs are plentiful, competition will continue to be stiff for the higher-paying supervisory jobs.

Certain technological developments—such as closed-circuit television, computer tracking systems, and automatic gates—do allow a single corrections officer to monitor a number of prisoners from a centralized location, but the impact of these technologies on overall staffing needs is minimal.

Crime Analysts

SUMMARY

Definition
Crime analysts analyze patterns in criminal behavior in order to catch criminals, predict patterns and motives of criminals, and improve the responsiveness of law enforcement agencies.

Alternative Job Titles
None

Salary Range
$25,000 to $45,000 to $60,000

Educational Requirements
Bachelor's degree

Certification or Licensing
Voluntary

Employment Outlook
Faster than the average

High School Subjects
Computer science
English (writing/literature)
Psychology
Sociology

Personal Interests
Computers
Figuring out how things work
Helping people: protection
Reading/books

A police radio drones in the background as crime analyst Metre Lewis quickly reads through crime reports from all of the area police stations. She is just beginning to type up a weekly report encapsulating the "hot" crime investigations when she hears something that catches her attention over the radio.

She shifts her chair to turn up the volume. Police officers from her department are investigating a report of a sexual assault, and the physical description of the perpetrator rings a bell. She remembers reading a report last week about a suspect with the same description (white male, stringy gray hair, and a tattoo of a snake on his right forearm) who was arrested on spousal abuse charges. Within minutes, she has sent his name, photograph, and last-known addresses to officers on the beat.

WHAT DOES A CRIME ANALYST DO?

Crime analysts try to uncover and piece together information about crime patterns, crime trends, and criminal suspects. It's a job that varies widely from day to day and from one law enforcement agency to the next. At its core is a systematic process that involves collecting, categorizing, analyzing, and sharing information in order to help the agency to better deploy officers on the street, work through difficult investigations, and increase arrests of criminals.

The basic work of a crime analyst involves collecting crime data from a range of sources, including police reports, statewide computer databases, crime newsletters, word-of-mouth tips, and interviews with suspects. This information is then analyzed for patterns. Crime analysts are constantly vigilant for details that are similar or familiar. In addition to specific crime data, a crime analyst might study general factors such as population density, the demographic makeup of the population, commuting patterns, economic conditions (average income, poverty level, job availability), effectiveness of law enforcement agencies, citizens' attitudes toward crime, and crime reporting practices.

The responsibilities of a crime analyst are often dependent upon the needs of their police department or law enforcement agency. One morning's tasks might include writing a profile on a particular demographic group's criminal patterns. On another day, an analyst could meet with the police chief to discuss an unusual string of local car thefts. Less frequently, the work includes going on "ride-alongs" with street cops or meeting with crime analysts from surrounding jurisdictions to exchange information about criminals who are plaguing the region. Occasionally, a crime analyst is pulled off of everyday responsibilities in order to work exclusively on a task force, usually focusing on a rash of violent crimes. As an ongoing responsibility, a crime analyst might be charged with tracking and monitoring "known offenders" (sex offenders, career criminals, repeat juvenile offenders, and parolees).

Lingo to Learn

cluster analysis A computerized analysis of where specific crimes are happening. This tool identifies crime "hot spots."

crime pattern The occurrence of similar crimes in a defined geographic area.

crime series A crime pattern where there is reason to believe that the same suspect is responsible for the crimes.

GIS Geographic information systems, a mapping software commonly used in crime analysis.

intelligence analysis The study of relationships between people, organizations, and events. This applies to organized crime, conspiratorial acts like money laundering, crime rings like auto theft or child pornography, or other crimes of corruption.

investigative analysis Sometimes referred to as criminal profiling, investigative analysis aids in the identification of the physical, psychological, emotional, and behavioral characteristics of serial rape and serial homicide suspects and may often provide an explanation as to "why" a person is committing these crimes.

MO: Modus operandi (method of operation); the manner in which a particular criminal commits a crime.

New computer technology has had a profound impact on the profession of crime analysis, helping it grow by leaps and bounds. In its earliest days, crime analysis simply meant gathering straight statistics on crime. Now these same statistics—coupled with specialized software—allow crime analysts to actually predict and prevent criminal activity.

The use of this analysis falls into three broad categories: tactical, strategic, and administrative. Tactical crime analysis aims at giving police officers and detectives prompt, in-the-field information that could lead to an arrest. These are the "hot" items that land on a crime analyst's desk, usually pertaining to specific crimes and offenders. For example, a criminal's method of operation (MO) can be studied in order to predict who the likely next targets or victims will be. The police can then set up stakeouts or saturate the area with patrol cars. Tactical analysis is also used to do crime-suspect correlation, which involves identifying suspects for certain crimes based on their criminal histories.

Strategic analysis deals with finding solutions to long-range problems and crime trends. For instance, a crime analyst could create a crime trend forecast, based on current and past criminal activity, using computer software. An analyst might also perform a "manpower deployment" study to see if the police department is making best use of its personnel. Another aspect of strategic analysis involves collating and disseminating demographic data on victims and geographic areas experiencing high crime

rates so that the police are able to beef up crime prevention efforts.

Lastly, administrative analysis helps to provide policy-making information to a police department's administration. This might include a statistical study on the activity levels of police officers that would support a request for hiring more officers. Administrative work could also include creating graphs and charts that are used in management presentations or writing a speech on local crime prevention to give to the city council.

WHAT IS IT LIKE TO BE A CRIME ANALYST?

Metre Lewis has been a crime analyst since 1986. She is currently employed by the Kissimmee Police Department in Kissimmee, Florida. Metre is also the cofounder and past president of the Florida Crime and Intelligence Analyst Association, and currently serves as its treasurer. "I am a one-person unit," she says, which makes for a busy workday. "Our agency is heavily involved in a CompStat-like process where criminal activity is reviewed against strategies that the department has employed to gauge the effectiveness of those strategies. My part in this process is pivotal. My day therefore starts with the review of all Part 1 Index Crimes. I compare them to past information to search for patterns and trends." Although Metre has a great deal of automation at her disposal, she still must read the reports to get a thorough understanding of what is going on. "Just because something is labeled an auto theft does not mean that it is really an auto theft," she explains.

Metre also uses a mapping program known as CrimeView to study the spatial relationship between incidents. She also reviews arrest information and field interrogation information for potential suspects. "This information is also disseminated to both our Patrol and Criminal Investigations Divisions," she says. "I am also responsible for supplying the public with statistical information in terms of crime hot spots. I field at least two calls per day requesting this type of information. I also review all incoming and outgoing flyers/bulletins from other agencies for relevance to activity within our jurisdiction. I am also responsible for generating a weekly report that is disseminated to patrol and to our criminal investigations division that highlights these Part 1 Crimes, and

To Be a Successful Crime Analyst, You Should . . .

- be inquisitive, logical, and have a very good memory for details
- have excellent research skills
- have a strong stomach for sometimes graphic or disturbing crime information
- be able to work as a member of a law enforcement team and not always be in the limelight

gives insights into the possible developing crime patterns."

DO I HAVE WHAT IT TAKES TO BE A CRIME ANALYST?

"Integrity, integrity, integrity," is Metre Lewis's response when asked to name the most important professional requirements for crime analysts. "You need a professional and personal level of integrity that will color all that you do. You must set the bar high for yourself, because few others will. You will need a level of commitment to doing the right thing, that says to others you are not to be toyed with."

A crime analyst also needs to be inquisitive and logical, and have a good memory for what he or she has heard and read. A willingness to dig in and do this sort of research is important, since much of the work involves piecing together disparate bits of information. Ask Steven Gottlieb, an internationally recognized crime analysis trainer, consultant, and executive director of the Alpha Group Center for Crime and Intelligence Analysis (one of the largest training providers of law enforcement analytical training in the world), just who will make a good crime analyst. He laughs and says, "Somebody who does crossword puzzles in ink." He explains that crime analysts love the process of working with bits of data that in and of themselves mean nothing. "It's only when you put them together that a clear picture emerges," he says. "I would also say that a good crime analyst would ideally have the intelligence of Einstein, the wisdom of Solomon, and the patience of Job."

Even though crime analysts aren't out on the streets, they're immersed in the law enforcement milieu and come into contact with information that's potentially disturbing. If you are the type of person who becomes especially upset after reading newspaper reports on a murder or a child's molestation, this might not be the right career for you.

It's important to note that a crime analyst has to be willing to work in the background and not always be in the limelight. The positive side is that a crime analyst plays a significant role in all of the big cases, but doesn't have to wear a bulletproof vest in 100-degree heat or direct traffic in the rain.

HOW DO I BECOME A CRIME ANALYST?

Education

High School

High school courses that will be especially useful to you in your career as a crime analyst include psychology, mathematics, computer science, and English. Psychology courses will help you learn more about human nature. A good foundation in algebra will help with statistics classes in college. A basic knowledge of computers, word processing, spreadsheets, and databases is important, as you will be using these tools every day in your work as a crime analyst. English classes will help you to become a better communicator. You may be writing reports or giving oral presentations to street cops, academics, or a city council.

Metre Lewis encourages students to take art and music classes. "When I used to give career presentations to high school students," she recalls, "I would tell them that they not only need science and math, which developed their critical thinking skills, but art and music as well. Why? Because art and music teach you to look at things differently, to look at things outside of the box, to interpret data in a variety of ways."

Postsecondary Training

The majority of agencies require a bachelor's degree for the position of crime analyst. Metre earned her bachelor's degree in criminal justice from Ohio State University. Other excellent degrees to consider include statistics, computer science, psychology, and sociology.

Certification or Licensing

Currently, only California offers a formal, state-sponsored certification program for crime analysts. "This certification program is the largest in the nation," Steven Gottlieb says, "and is currently the only certification in the world regulated by state government law enforcement oversight that offers a government-issued certificate to graduates of any state, province, or country who successfully complete the curriculum. It is for this reason that this particular certification program is so valued and well regarded today." Steven was a key figure in establishing the certification program, which is supported by the California Department of Justice. After participating on several hiring panels, he says it became clear that some of the people applying for positions as crime analysts had solid experience in related areas, but could benefit from focused training in crime analysis.

The first university to offer the certification program was California State University–Fullerton. Currently, the program is offered at California State University campuses in Fullerton, Northridge, and Sacramento, and at the University of California–Riverside. To be certified, a person takes 36 to 40 hours of courses. The curriculum focuses on crime analysis, criminal intelligence analysis, investigative analysis, and law enforcement research methods and statistics. Certification also requires completion of prerequisite courses in criminal law and criminal justice, demonstrated competency in the use of computer software, and 400 hours of work experience, which is earned by volunteer service in the crime or intelligence analysis unit of a federal, state, or municipal law enforcement agency.

Steven says that the importance of certification cannot be overemphasized. "Police administrators know," he says, "that when they hire a certified crime analyst they are hiring someone who has actually demonstrated, to the satisfaction of independent third parties (their instructors, the universities, and the California Department of Justice), their ability to perform competently on the job. Further, they know that they are hiring an individual who has had formal analytical training and who possesses

Crime Confusion

In a field like crime analysis, there's sometimes confusion about who does what. So, here are a few professions with titles that might sound a lot like crime analyst, but are actually different careers.

Crime scene evidence technicians go to the scene of the crime in order to collect and photograph relevant evidence, such as fingerprints, hairs, bullets, etc.

Criminalists scientifically analyze, compare, and evaluate physical evidence in the laboratory.

Criminal intelligence analysts study the relationships between people, organizations, and events. They often focus on organized crime, money laundering, and other conspiratorial crimes.

Criminologists study and research crime from a sociological perspective. They usually work in a university setting, rather than for a law enforcement agency.

Forensic psychologists make psychological evaluations based on criminal evidence or behavior.

Investigative analysts attempt to uncover why a person is committing serial crimes such as murder and rape. Getting into the field of investigative analysis (sometimes called "profiling") usually requires years of experience and additional education in psychology—as well as good instincts.

the knowledge, skills, and abilities to provide useful products and services to the officers, investigators, and administrators of their departments. In short, administrators know that by hiring a certified crime analyst they're not hiring a pig in a poke, but someone who is poised to make a meaningful contribution to their agencies."

Internships and Volunteerships

An internship during college is the best way to get a foot in the door and gain on-the-job experience. As a result of lean staffing, many units rely on interns to provide basic support such as performing clerical duties, as well as reading police reports and learning how to glean significant facts and patterns from them.

There are plenty of ways that you can begin your own training and education now. First of all, get some exposure to the law enforcement community by volunteering at the local police department. Many towns have a Boy Scouts Explorers program in which students (of both sexes) work and take mini-courses in law enforcement.

WHO WILL HIRE ME?

Metre Lewis says that she was very blessed in getting her first position as a crime analyst. "I was working as a dispatcher for the Orlando Police Department when the department decided to start a crime analysis unit. They hired the three most dynamic women ever to form a crime analysis unit. The rest is history."

The majority of crime analysts are employed by local and state law enforcement agencies. A great number are also hired by federal agencies such as the Federal Bureau of Investigation; the U.S. Secret Service; Alcohol, Tobacco, and Firearms; Immigration and Customs Enforcement;

and the Department of Justice. In addition, some private security firms, insurance companies, and major retailers hire people with training in crime analysis.

While there's not a single, central clearinghouse for all crime or intelligence analyst jobs, there are several places to look for listings. For example, job openings are posted on the Web sites of the California Crime and Intelligence Analysts Association (http://www.crimeanalyst.org), the International Association of Law Enforcement Intelligence Analysts (http://www.ialeia.net), and the International Association of Crime Analysts (http://iaca.net/JobOps.asp).

WHERE CAN I GO FROM HERE?

As a broad generalization, most crime analysts are not pushing and shoving to climb the career ladder. Since theirs is often a one- or two-person, non-hierarchical unit within an agency, they more likely chose crime analysis because they relish the nature of the work itself. Obviously, advancement possibilities depend largely on the size and structure of the agency for which a crime analyst works. In larger agencies, there are sometimes senior analysts, supervising analysts, or crime analysis managers. Some of these positions require a master's degree.

WHAT ARE THE SALARY RANGES?

Earnings for crime analysts vary considerably, based on factors such as the

Related Jobs

- crime scene evidence technicians
- criminal intelligence analysts
- criminalists
- criminologists
- detectives
- FBI agents
- forensic psychologists
- intelligence officers
- investigative analysts
- medical examiners
- police officers

location, the size of the employing agency and its financial status, and the analyst's experience. The International Association of Crime Analysts reports that salaries range from $25,000 to $60,000 per year. Analysts receive the same benefits as others working in the same agency. These usually include paid vacation time, sick leave, health insurance, and retirement plans.

WHAT IS THE JOB OUTLOOK?

In recent times, there has been a tremendous surge of interest in the field of crime analysis. One factor has been the emergence of community-oriented policing. This concept strives to get police officers out on the streets of their communities, rather than sitting at a desk. "With a limited number of officers, departments have to ask, 'What's the best use of their time?'" says Steven Gottlieb. "Good crime analysis helps to deploy officers in the right places at the right times."

Steven agrees that the future employment outlook for crime and intelligence analysts is very good. "Crime and intelligence analysts are now employed throughout all levels of government (federal, state, and municipal)," he says. "With the horrific events of 9/11 came an increasing realization that law enforcement needs specially trained people who can analyze the vast amounts of data gathered by officers and investigators and use it to create an accurate assessment of crime in their communities. As a result, law enforcement administrators are better able to police their jurisdictions on the basis of objective facts rather than mere perceptions."

The field is also growing because better software is becoming available. "When I started in the business 23 years ago," Steven says, "all we had was a desk, a yellow pad, and good intentions. Today we have a formalized process for analyzing crime and the assistance of computers, automated information systems, mapping software, the Internet, and the ability to obtain information from our counterparts throughout the world at lightning speed.

While this growth trend is expected to continue, it's important to recognize that it is still a competitive job market. Those who want to become crime analysts should be willing to move to find an agency with a job opening. They should also bear in mind that police departments are historically more likely to lay off a civilian than a street officer.

Emergency Medical Technicians

SUMMARY

Definition
Emergency medical technicians give immediate first aid treatment to sick or injured persons both at the scene and en route to the hospital or other medical facility. They also make sure that the emergency vehicle—an ambulance or a helicopter—is stocked with the necessary supplies and is in good operating condition.

Alternative Job Titles
Paramedics

Salary Range
$16,000 to $25,000 to $43,000+

Educational Requirements
Some postsecondary training

Certification or Licensing
Required

Employment Outlook
Much faster than the average

High School Subjects
Anatomy and physiology
Biology
Health
Physical education

Personal Interests
Helping people: physical health/medicine
Helping people: protection

The care of an emergency medical technician (EMT) often can mean the difference between life and death. Acute congestive heart failure is just one condition that paramedic Connie Meyer encounters often. "This happens to someone with ongoing cardiac problems who suddenly develops shortness of breath," she explains. "It can happen in a matter of 10 or 15 minutes and is definitely life threatening." Connie says that even a basic EMT can make a tremendous difference to this type of patient by assisting his or her breathing with a device called a bag valve mask, which fits over the mouth and helps the patient breathe while he or she is still awake. "Advanced EMTs or paramedics can administer IV medications to help move the fluids out of the lungs," she says, "and, during the time of transport to the hospital, we can take an acutely ill patient from drowning in his or her own fluids to sitting up with no apparent distress.

"This is one of our more dramatic types of calls, but, in reality, the most common thing we do to help our patients is provide a helping hand and kind word in a situation in which they feel completely out of control. Calming and reassuring our patients is something we do on every call, and, I believe, the most important thing that every EMT and paramedic does on a daily basis."

WHAT DOES AN EMERGENCY MEDICAL TECHNICIAN DO?

If you are sick or hurt, you usually go to a doctor; if you are very sick or hurt, you may go to the emergency room of a local hospital. But what if you are alone and unable to drive, or you are too badly injured to travel without receiving medical treatment first? It often happens that an accident or injury victim needs on-the-spot help and safe, rapid transportation to the hospital. *Emergency medical technicians*, or *EMTs*, are the ones who fill this need.

Emergency medical technicians respond to emergency situations to give immediate attention to people who need it. Whether employed by a hospital, police department, fire department, or private ambulance company, the EMT crew functions as a traveling arm of the emergency room. While on duty, an EMT could be called out for car accidents, heart attacks, work-related injuries, or drug overdoses. He or she might help deliver a baby, treat the victim of a gunshot wound, or revive a child who has nearly drowned. In short, EMTs may find themselves in almost any circumstance that could be called a medical crisis.

Usually working in teams of two, EMTs receive their instructions from the emergency medical dispatcher, who has taken the initial call for help, and drive to the scene in an ambulance. (Some EMTs fly in helicopters to accident or trauma scenes and transport their patient by air to the hospital.) The dispatcher will remain in contact with the EMT crew through a two-way radio link. This allows the EMTs to relay important information about the emergency scene and the victims and to receive any further instructions, either from the dispatcher or from a medical staff member, if need be. Since they are usually the first trained medical help on the scene, it is very important that they be able to evaluate the situation and make good, logical judgments about what should be done in what order, as well as what should not be done at all. By observing the victim's injuries or symptoms, looking for medic alert tags, and asking the necessary questions, the EMTs determine what action to take and then begin first aid treatment. Some more complicated procedures may require the EMT to be in radio contact with hospital staff, who can give step-by-step directions.

The types of treatments an individual is able to give depend mostly on the level of training and certification he or she has completed. First responders, the lowest tier of workers in the emergency services, are qualified to provide basic care to the sick and injured since they are often the first to arrive on scene during an emergency. This designation is often held by firefighters, police officers, and other emergency services workers. The most common designation that EMTs hold is EMT-basic. A basic EMT can perform

Lingo to Learn

advanced life support Intensive treatment options—such as giving IVs, administering medications, and monitoring heart rhythms—that are provided by an emergency medical services worker who has attained the rank of EMT-paramedic.

AMKUS cutter A handheld rescue device, similar to scissors, used to free trapped victims by cutting through metal.

AMKUS rams A handheld rescue device used to free trapped victims by pushing or pulling obstructions, such as dashboard and seats, away from the victim.

AMKUS spreader A handheld rescue device used to free trapped victims by pulling crumpled metal apart.

backboard A long, flat, hard surface used to immobilize the spine in the case of neck or spinal injury.

basic life support Treatment options that can be provided by an emergency medical services worker who has attained the rank of EMT-basic. These include providing oxygen, monitoring pulse and respirations, bandaging wounds, and applying splints.

cardiac arrest The complete stoppage of the heartbeat.

defibrillator An apparatus consisting of alternating currents of electricity, with electrodes to apply the currents to heart muscles in order to shock the muscles into operation. Requires the operator to interpret the heart rhythms and to apply the shock at the proper time.

endotracheal intubation The insertion of a tube into the trachea, or windpipe, to provide a passage for the air, in case of obstruction.

IV Intravenous, administered by an injection into the vein.

CPR, control bleeding, treat shock victims, apply bandages, splint fractures, and perform automatic defibrillation, which requires no interpretation of EKGs. Such an EMT is also trained to deal with emotionally disturbed patients and heart attack, poisoning, and burn victims. The EMT-intermediate, which is the second level of training, is also prepared to start an IV, if needed, or to use a manual defibrillator to apply electrical shocks to the heart in the case of a cardiac arrest. A growing number of EMTs are choosing to train for the highest level of certification—the EMT-paramedic. With this certification, the individual is permitted to perform more intensive treatment procedures. Often working in close radio contact with a doctor, he or she may give drugs intravenously or orally, interpret EKGs, perform endotracheal intubation, and use more complex life-support equipment.

In a case where a victim or victims are trapped, EMTs first give medical treatment, and then remove the victim, using special equipment such as the AMKUS Power Unit. They may need to work closely with the police or the fire department in the rescue attempt.

If patients must be taken from the emergency scene to the hospital, the EMTs may place them on a backboard or stretcher, then carry and lift them into the ambulance. One EMT drives to the hospital, while the other monitors the passenger's vital signs and provides any necessary care. One of them must notify the hospital emergency room, either directly or through the dispatcher, of how many people are coming in and the type of injuries they have. They also may record the blood pressure, pulse, present condition, and any medical history they know, in order to assist the hospital.

Once at the hospital, the EMTs help the staff bring in the patient or patients, and assist with any necessary first steps of in-hospital treatment. They then provide their observations to the hospital staff, as well as information about the treatment they have given at the scene and on the way to the hospital.

Finally, each run must also be documented by the acting EMTs for the records of the provider. Once the run is over, the EMTs are responsible for restocking the ambulance, sterilizing equipment, replacing dirty linens, and making sure that everything is in order for the next run. For the EMT crews to function efficiently and quickly, they must ensure that they have all the equipment and supplies they need, and that the ambulance itself is clean, properly maintained, and filled with gas.

WHAT IS IT LIKE TO BE AN EMT?

Connie Meyer has been an emergency medical technician for 23 years. She works as a paramedic captain for the Johnson County Med-Act in Olathe, Kansas. "We respond to a variety of calls," she says, "but many of them are related to heart problems, strokes, and diabetes. Unfortunately, a large number also are related to drug and/or alcohol use—either directly from overdoses and accidents related to use, or related to medical problems caused by the drug and alcohol use. Many of our patients also have underlying mental problems."

Connie works in what is called a "partnership" unit, meaning, she explains, "that I am employed by the county and my paramedic partner is employed by the city fire department."

On a typical day, Connie arrives at the ambulance station 15 to 20 minutes before the start of her shift. "We are housed in a fire station and receive a report from the off-going crew," she says. "Then we check the ambulance and equipment each morning to assure everything is there and working properly. When a 911 call comes in to the dispatch center, a computer-aided dispatch program chooses which ambulance is closest, and we are sent to the call. We respond with the police department and fire crews to some calls. After evaluation and necessary stabilization on scene, patients are transported to their hospital of choice unless a closer hospital is deemed necessary for better care."

Between calls, Connie and her coworkers wait in the fire station. Complete with sleeping quarters, a kitchen, and a living area, as well as an office area for work, it has a comfortable atmosphere.

In addition to responding to calls, Connie must complete other duties, including some type of EMS training. "One day each month we report to mandatory training sessions that last two to three hours," she explains. "These sessions cover a variety of EMS-related topics and hands-on training."

EMT work can be physically demanding. EMTs often work outside, in any type of weather, and most of their time on a run is spent standing, kneeling, bending, and lifting. It is also stressful and often emotionally draining. Connie works 10 24-hour shifts each month. "The 24 hours can be *very* long if it is a busy day and night, and you get no sleep," she says. The nature of an EMT shift depends almost entirely on how many and what type of calls come in. Some shifts are incredibly busy, although not all of those are emergency runs. "The ambulance I work on runs, on average, 7 to 13 calls during the 24-hour period," Connie says.

Asked what she likes most about her job, Connie cites the variety of tasks that EMTs are able to perform. "We work within a set of protocols and standing orders and can do most lifesaving tasks without contacting medical control first," she says. "The nature of a call can vary widely, and I like that variety in my job as well as the independence of the work."

Some emergency medical technicians, such as Karen Kellogg, who is employed by the Overland Park Fire Department in Overland Park, Kansas, work as both EMTs

and firefighters. As a firefighter/EMT she fights fires, works non-fire-related calls, and responds to calls that require her emergency medical training. "Our [EMT] calls are typically cyclic," she says. "In humid weather and cold weather we run a lot of difficulty breathing calls; in hot weather there are many heat-related injuries; in icy weather we run a lot of falls and motor vehicle accidents; we run many motor vehicle accidents in wet weather, too. If there are a lot of nursing or assisted-living homes in the area we run a variety of chronic illness calls. In areas with an aging population where people live alone, we run a lot of calls mostly in the middle of the night to people who are lonely and just need someone to talk to. On holidays

To Be a Successful Emergency Medical Technician, You Should . . .

- have a desire to serve people
- be emotionally stable and clearheaded
- have good manual dexterity and agility
- have strong written and oral communication skills
- be able to lift and carry up to 125 pounds
- have good eyesight and color vision

we run lots of heart patients and code blues (a patient who has no pulse and no respirations)."

DO I HAVE WHAT IT TAKES TO BE AN EMT?

Connie Meyer says that to be successful in this field, EMTs must have empathy, flexibility, and curiosity. "If EMTs do not have empathy for their patients," she explains, "burnout will quickly develop as they get frustrated with the 'minor' calls instead of every patient being critically ill and in need of the EMT's help. Only a small portion of our patients have a critical problem at the time they call 911, but all need help of some type. We just have to figure out what they need and try to fill that need. Flexibility is important because patients rarely present like the textbook says they should. We have to adapt to each situation as it develops and improvise as necessary to provide the best care. Curiosity also plays into this because we have to go beneath the surface sometimes to figure out what is really going on. An EMT can just be a taxi ride to the hospital, but if EMTs are there to truly help the patient, they must first figure out what is wrong."

Karen Kellogg, who has been an EMT for 15 years, believes that EMTs "need the ability to quickly assess a patient by observing their appearance and asking good questions; the ability to adapt to a variety of situations (there are few textbook calls); and the ability to deliver compassionate care to all patients (not all people are equally pleasant to treat) while maintaining a degree of professional detachment."

EMTs regularly encounter situations that many people would find upsetting. Because they are faced with unpleasant scenes, crises, and even death, they need a certain emotional capability for coping. They must have stable personalities and be able to keep their heads in circumstances of extreme stress. It's important that the EMT be able to cope with such bad experiences without suffering lasting negative results. The stress and the emotional strain can take its toll; there is a high turnover rate in the EMS field.

Another important skill in this profession is the ability to work closely with others. Partners have to rely heavily on each other and communicate easily and well to be a good emergency team.

HOW DO I BECOME AN EMERGENCY MEDICAL TECHNICIAN?

Education

Connie Meyer prepared for her career by taking an EMT class at a community college. "After the class was completed, I took a written and practical test to be certified to work on the ambulance in my state," she recalls. "I worked as a volunteer EMT for the hospital I was employed with for a number of years, then was hired by a county-run EMS agency, which paid for me to attend paramedic school (a college certificate program)." Connie's state (Kansas) has now changed the requirements for becoming a parademic, so programs award an associate's degree. "I completed the requirements for my associate's degree two years after completing paramedic class," Connie says. "Paramedics must also take a written and practical test; mine was a state test but, currently, the test is through the National Registry of Emergency Medical Technicians."

High School

A high school diploma, or its equivalent, is required for admission into the EMT training program. While most high school studies will not yield experience with emergency medical care, health classes may offer a good introduction to some of the concepts and terms used by EMTs. It may also be possible to take courses in first aid or CPR through your local Red Cross or other organizations. This sort of training can be valuable, giving you advance preparation for the actual EMT program. Some science classes, such as anatomy, can also be helpful, in that you can become familiar with the human body and its various systems.

Driver's education is recommended as well for anyone who is interested in a career as an EMT. The ability to drive safely and sensibly in all different types of road conditions, and a firm knowledge of traffic laws, is essential to the driver of an ambulance. English is a desirable subject for the potential EMT, since it is important to have good communication skills, both written and oral, along with the capacity to read and interpret well. Finally, depending on what area of the country you might work in, it can be very helpful to have a background in a foreign language, such as Spanish, to assist in dealing with patients who speak little or no English.

Postsecondary Training

For the high school graduate with a strong interest in the emergency medical services, the next step is formal training. The standard training course was designed by the U.S. Department of Transportation and is often offered by police, fire, and health departments. It may also be offered by hospitals or as a nondegree course in colleges, particularly community colleges.

The program teaches EMTs-to-be how to deal with many common emergencies. The student will learn how to deal with bleeding, cardiac arrest, childbirth, broken bones, and choking. He or she will also become familiar with the specialized equipment used in many emergency situations, like backboards, stretchers, fracture kits, splints, and oxygen systems.

If you live in an area that offers several different courses, it might be a good idea to research all the options, since certain courses may emphasize different aspects of the job. After completing the basic course, there are training sessions available to teach more specialized skills, such as removing trapped victims, driving an ambulance, or dispatching.

Certification or Licensing

After the training program has been successfully completed, the graduate has the opportunity to work toward becoming certified or registered with the National Registry of Emergency Medical Technicians (NREMT) (see "Look to the Pros" in Section 4: What Can I Do Now?). All states have some sort of certification requirement of their own, but many of them accept registration in NREMT in place of their own certification. Applicants should check the specific regulations and requirements for their state.

At present, the NREMT recognizes four levels of competency: first responder, EMT-basic, EMT-intermediate, and EMT-paramedic. Although it is not always essential for EMTs to become registered with one of these ratings, you can expect better job prospects as you attain higher levels of registration.

Candidates for the first responder designation must have completed the standard Department of Transportation training program (or their state's equivalent) and pass both a state-approved practical examination and a written examination.

Candidates for the EMT-basic designation must have completed the standard Department of Transportation training program (or their state's equivalent), have six months' experience, have a current approved CPR credential for the professional rescuer, and pass both a state-approved practical examination and a written examination.

The EMT-intermediate level of competency requires all candidates to have current registration at the EMT-basic level. They must also have a certain amount of experience, have a current approved CPR credential for the professional rescuer, and pass both a written test and a practical examination.

To become an EMT-paramedic, or EMT-P, the highest level of registration, candidates must already be registered at the basic or intermediate level. They must have completed a special EMT-P training program and pass both a written and practical examination. Because training is much more comprehensive and specialized than for other EMTs, EMT-Ps are prepared to make more physician-like observations and judgments.

Internships and Volunteerships

As part of your EMT training program, you will have the opportunity to participate in an internship in a hospital emergency room, with a fire or emergency services department, or in another health care setting. Volunteer opportunities in which you provide support (filing, counting supplies, cleaning gear, etc.) may also be available. Contact your local emergency services department for more information.

Labor Unions

Some EMTs may have the opportunity to join a union when they become employed, especially if they work for a municipal fire, police, or rescue department. EMTs with membership in a union pay weekly or monthly dues, and receive in return a package of services designed to improve working conditions, which include collective bargaining for pay and benefits, governmental lobbying, and legal representation.

WHO WILL HIRE ME?

Before Connie Meyer became an EMT, she worked in the health care field for

Advancement Possibilities

● ● ● ● ● ● ●

Emergency medical services coordinators direct medical emergency service programs, coordinate emergency staff, maintain records, develop and participate in training programs for rescue personnel, cooperate with community organizations to promote knowledge of and to provide training in first aid, and work with emergency services in other areas to coordinate activities and area plans.

Physician assistants work under the direction and responsibility of physicians to provide health care to patients: examine patients; perform or order diagnostic tests; give necessary injections, immunizations, suturing, and wound care; develop patient management plans; and counsel patients in following prescribed medical regimens.

Training directors plan and oversee continuing education for rescue personnel, design and implement quality assurance programs, and develop and direct specialized training courses or sessions for rescue personnel.

some time as a medical transcriptionist and business manager of a small hospital. "The hospital had a volunteer ambulance and needed EMTs," she recalls. "I took the EMT class because I could easily respond to calls during the day and not have to leave a patient behind. After a few years, I had the opportunity to work full time as an EMT, and my service paid for me to attend paramedic school."

Karen Kellogg applied for a firefighter/ EMT opening advertised by the fire department and took and passed its written, psychological, and physical fitness tests. "I was already FF- and EMT-certified as required by the department," she explains. "It was my first and is still my only job in the field."

There are approximately 192,000 EMTs and paramedics employed in the United States. Most EMTs work for private ambulance services; municipal fire, police, or rescue departments; and hospitals or medical centers. Also, there are many who volunteer, particularly in more rural areas, where there often are no paid EMTs at all.

Because new graduates will be in heavy competition for full-time employment, it may be easier to break into the field on a part-time or volunteer basis. By beginning as a volunteer or part-timer, you can gain hours of valuable experience, which can be useful in landing a paid, full-time position later. The competition is also stiffer for beginning EMTs in the public sector, such as police and fire departments. Beginners may have more success in finding a position in a private ambulance company. There are also opportunities for work that lie somewhat off the beaten path. For example, many industrial plants have EMTs in their safety departments, and security companies sometimes prefer to hire EMTs for their staff. Most amusement parks and other public attractions employ EMTs in their first aid stations, and in many cities there are private companies that hire EMTs to provide medical services for concerts, fairs, sporting events, and other gatherings.

One good source of employment leads is the school or agency that provided your training. Job openings may sometimes be listed in the newspaper classifieds under "Emergency Medical Technician," "EMT," "Emergency Medical Services," "Ambulance Technician," "Rescue Squad," or "Health Care." It may be worthwhile for students nearing the end of their training course to subscribe to a local paper. Also, many professional journals and national and state EMS newsletters list openings.

It is also a good idea to apply directly to local ambulance services, hospitals, fire departments, and police departments in your area. The best approach is usually to send a current résumé, complete with references, and a letter of inquiry. The letter should consist of a brief description of your situation and interests, and a request for an application. Most agencies have specific applications and employment procedures, so the résumé and cover letter alone are not necessarily adequate. It is important to remember that most employers will accept applications to keep on file even if there is no specific job open at the time.

WHERE CAN I GO FROM HERE?

For an EMT who is interested in advancement, the first move is usually to become certified as a paramedic. Once at that level, there are further opportunities in the area of administration. Moving into an admin-

istrative position usually means leaving fieldwork and patient care for a more routine office job. An EMT-paramedic can pursue such positions as supervisor, operations manager, administrative director, or executive director of emergency services. Or, he or she may be interested in a career in education and training. There are also several new areas of specialization in EMS. Quality control, safety and risk management, communications, and flight operations are some examples of these up-and-coming administrative areas.

Some EMTs move out of health care entirely and into sales and marketing of emergency medical equipment. Often, their experience and familiarity with the field make them effective and valuable salespeople. Finally, some EMTs decide to go back to school and become registered nurses, physicians, or other types of health workers.

Connie Meyer is eligible to retire in five years. "I haven't decided whether this is my plan, yet," she says, "because I still really enjoy working on the ambulance. It is also a possibility that I will become a field supervisor (battalion chief) within my system, where I can still run calls, but it would not be as physically demanding as daily work on the ambulance." Karen Kellogg plans to retire in 5 years after reaching 20 years with her department. "The job requirements for a FF/EMT are extremely physically demanding—especially for a woman," she says. "Although I am able to perform my job-related duties currently, it has become increasingly difficult as I have gotten older. I am concerned that I will be physically unable to maintain the necessary performance level beyond the next five years."

WHAT ARE THE SALARY RANGES?

Earnings of EMTs depend on the type of employer and the individual level of training and experience. Those working in the public sector (for police and fire departments) usually receive a higher wage than those working in the private sector (for ambulance companies and hospitals). Salary levels typically rise with greater skill, training, and certification. According to the U.S. Department of Labor, median annual earnings of EMTs and paramedics were $25,310 in 2004. Salaries ranged from less than $16,090 to more than $43,240.

Benefits vary widely, depending on the employer, but generally include uniform allowance, paid holidays and vacations, health insurance, and pension plans.

Related Jobs

- ambulance attendants
- birth attendants
- chiropractor's assistants
- dental assistants
- first aid attendants
- licensed practical nurses
- medical assistants
- nursing assistants
- occupational therapy aides and assistants
- optometric assistants
- orderlies
- orthopedic assistants
- physical therapy aides and assistants
- physician assistants
- podiatric assistants
- psychiatric aides
- registered nurses
- surgical technicians

WHAT IS THE JOB OUTLOOK?

Employment opportunities for EMTs are expected to grow much faster than the average for all occupations through 2014, according to the U.S. Department of Labor. "EMTs will continue to provide a vital emergency medical service," says Karen Kellogg. "EMT roles are expanding as local medical societies develop a broader understanding of the span of skills that can be performed at a basic life support level."

Another reason for this growth is simply that the population is growing, thus creating the need for more medical personnel. Another factor is that the proportion of elderly people, who are the biggest users of emergency medical services, is growing in many communities. Finally, many jobs will become available because, as noted earlier, the EMT profession does have a high turnover rate. "There is an ongoing shortage of EMTs and paramedics throughout the country," says Connie

Meyer. This happens for a variety of reasons. In the areas where EMS Services depend on volunteers, it is becoming harder to retain volunteers who must choose between their volunteer jobs and one that pays them so they can continue to pay their bills. In the paid services like mine, which is county run, we have a constant competition from the fire service to hire paramedics for more money. Other EMTs and paramedics leave the field to continue a health care career, but in other fields such as nursing or medical school."

The job opportunities for the individual EMT will depend partly upon the community in which he or she wishes to work. In the larger, more metropolitan areas, where the majority of paid EMT positions are available, the opportunities will probably be best. In many smaller communities, financial difficulties are causing many not-for-profit hospitals and municipal police, fire, and rescue squads to cut back on staff. Because of this, there are likely to be fewer job possibilities in the public sector. However, since many of the organizations suffering cutbacks opt to contract with a private ambulance company for service to their community, opportunities with these private companies may increase.

The trend toward private ambulance companies, which have historically paid less, is an important one, as it is likely to influence where the jobs can be found, as well as what the average pay is. One reason for the growth of the private ambulance industry is a health care reform concept called managed care. As health care costs increase, more Americans are leaving their private health care plans for "pool" systems, which provide health care for large groups. The reason this affects the EMT profession is that medical transportation is one of the major services typically contracted for by these pool systems, or managed care providers. As managed care gains popularity, there is a greater need for the private ambulance contractors.

Because of America's growing concern about health care costs, the person considering a career as an EMT should be aware that health care reforms may affect all medical professions to some extent. Also, as mentioned before, the increase and growth of private ambulance services will almost definitely change the face of the emergency services field. In looking at a future as an emergency medical technician, both of these factors are worth keeping in mind.

FBI Agents

SUMMARY

Definition
Agents for the Federal Bureau of Investigation are responsible for investigating and enforcing more than 200 federal statutes that encompass terrorism, organized crime, white-collar crime, public corruption, financial crime, government fraud, bribery, copyright matters, civil rights violations, bank robbery, extortion, kidnapping, air piracy, terrorism, foreign counterintelligence, interstate criminal activity, and fugitive and drug trafficking matters.

Alternative Job Titles
Special agents

Salary Range
$41,000 to $64,000 to $100,000+

Educational Requirements
Bachelor's degree

Employment Outlook
About as fast as the average

High School Subjects
Computer science
Foreign language
Mathematics
Physical education
Psychology

Personal Interests
Computers
Current events
Exercise/personal fitness
Helping people: protection
Law
Psychology
Reading/books

"The most interesting days I've ever had in the FBI were the days following September 11, 2001," says John Diwik, an FBI special agent for 18 years. "I heard about the attack while driving to work. Upon arriving at the office everyone was spellbound as we watched the news on television. Almost immediately, the FBI ramped up an amazing investigation of the terrorists. We worked 24-7 for six months. Everyone dug in, everyone worked hard, everyone gave that little bit extra and pulled together. I hope we never experience anything like it again, but it shows how dedicated and capable we are."

WHAT DOES AN FBI AGENT DO?

Formed in 1908, the FBI has the broadest investigative authority of all federal law enforcement agencies. The agency leads long-term, complex investigations, while working closely with other federal, state, local, and foreign law enforcement and intelligence agencies.

An FBI special agent is faced with the challenge of investigating and upholding certain federal laws that come under the FBI's jurisdictions. Throughout their career, FBI agents conduct investigations on a variety of issues that are lumped into the following categories: counterterrorism, counterintelligence, cyber investigations, public corruption, civil rights, organized crime, white-collar crime (such as antitrust investigations, bankruptcy fraud, environmental crime, financial institution fraud, government fraud, health care fraud, insurance fraud, money laundering, securities/commodities fraud, and telemarketing fraud), and major thefts/violent crimes (such as art theft, crimes against children, jewelry and gem theft, and Indian Country crime). FBI agents may be assigned to a wide range of investigations, unless they have specialized skills in a certain area. In short, agents are assigned to a case, conduct an investigation, and then submit a report of their findings to the U.S. Attorney's Office.

During an investigation, agents may use a vast network of communication systems and the bureau's crime detection laboratory to help them with their work. Agents may gather information with the help of the National Crime Information Center and the Criminal Justice Information Services Division. Once they have information, agents must make sure the facts and evidence are correct. FBI agents may discuss their findings with a U.S. attorney or an assistant U.S. attorney, who decides whether the evidence requires legal action. The Justice Depart-

Lingo to Learn

MO: Modus operandi (method of operation); the standard pattern that an individual typically uses to commit a crime.

profile A general description of a type of person who might commit a certain kind of crime. For example, the FBI creates profiles of serial killers and financial criminals.

special agent A government title for federal employees who investigate criminal violations.

street agent An FBI agent not in management who conducts investigations.

surveillance Following, observing, or listening to people.

wiretap Electronic surveillance over the telephone.

ment may choose to investigate the matter further, and the FBI agents may obtain a search warrant or court order to locate and seize property that may be evidence. If the Justice Department decides to prosecute the case, the agent may then obtain an arrest warrant.

With the goal of gathering information and reporting it, FBI agents may spend a considerable amount of time traveling to or living in various cities. Their investigations often require the agent to interview people—witnesses, subjects, or suspects—and search for different types of records. Agents may set up a stakeout to watch a place or person. Special agents may also work with paid informants. Sometimes agents testify in court about their investigations or findings. If enough incriminating evidence is found, FBI agents conduct arrests or raids of various types. Agents must carry firearms while on duty, and they typically carry their bureau identification badge. Agents always carry their credentials. Most of the time they wear everyday business suits or other appropriate attire—not uniforms.

Some agents with specialized skills may work specific types of investigations, such as fraud or embezzlement. *Language specialists*—who can be employed as special agents or support personnel—may translate foreign language over a wiretap and tape recordings into English. The FBI also employs agents specializing in areas such as chemistry, physics, metallurgy, or computers. *Laboratory specialists* analyze physical evidence like blood, hair, and body fluids, while others analyze handwriting, documents, and firearms. Agents working for the FBI's Behavioral Science Unit track and profile serial murderers, rapists, and other criminals committing patterned violent crimes.

Agents often work alone, unless the investigation is particularly dangerous or requires more agents. However, FBI agents do not investigate local matters—only federal violations that fall within their jurisdiction. The agents' work can be discussed only with other bureau employees, which means they cannot discuss investigations with their families or friends.

The FBI operates 56 field offices, 400 resident agencies, 4 specialized field installations, and 46 foreign liaison posts.

FBI agents must be willing to be reassigned at any point in their career.

WHAT IS IT LIKE TO BE AN FBI AGENT?

Special Agent John Diwik has been an FBI agent since July of 1987. "I've been assigned to the Chicago Division for my entire career. I came into the bureau in New Haven, Connecticut, and was immediately assigned to Chicago after graduation from the FBI Academy."

John works on one of the Public Corruption squads in the FBI's Chicago Division. According to the FBI's Web site, "public corruption investigations focus on all levels of government (local, state, and federal) and include allegations of judicial, legislative, regulatory, contract, and law enforcement corruption." John's typical day begins at 8:00 A.M. He checks his mail folder and e-mails and determines what tasks he will focus on during his workday. "Some days I may review documentary evidence for an entire day," he says. Typically, I might also create an Excel spreadsheet or a report to memorialize the documents I have reviewed. Some days I may be on the computer doing public database searches to obtain information on my subjects/witnesses. Some days are spent typing reports of interviews. Some days are spent conducting interviews throughout the Chicago metro area. Many hours are spent drafting subpoena requests, which are submitted to the United States Attorney's Office. Once they are created, I may spend considerable time serving the subpoenas in person, via fax, or by mail." John also spends significant time in meetings with Assistant United States Attorneys (AUSAs). "If I have a trial coming up," he says, "I may spend days or months working on organizing evidence, meeting with AUSAs, or doing pretrial witness interviews. Preparing for a trial is probably the most tedious work an agent does."

John also occasionally participates in squad meetings where his supervisor addresses various topics. He might also be required to provide brief summaries of cases he is working on or to discuss an upcoming search or arrest. "Occasionally," John adds, "we attend training seminars on a variety of topics from interrogation and computer training, to evidence recovery and conducting financial investigations. Training may be very informal and in our office, or it may involve traveling to a seminar at Quantico, Virginia, or to the National Advocacy Center in Columbia, South Carolina. In general, most agents don't travel that much. Once in a while, casework requires that we travel to conduct an important interview. I personally travel fairly frequently to conduct training seminars and to make speeches. I have extensive experience investigating bankruptcy fraud (and other financial frauds) and conducting financial investigations. I typically make presentations to other federal agencies or the business community."

Work as an FBI agent can be intense and sometimes draining. While all agents must work a minimum of 50 hours a week—sometimes 70 hours a week—they

A Short History of the FBI

The FBI was founded in 1908 to serve as the investigative arm of the U.S. Department of Justice. In the early years, agents investigated federal violations such as bankruptcy frauds, antitrust crime, and neutrality violations. During World War I, the bureau began investigating espionage, sabotage, sedition, and draft violations. In 1932, kidnapping became a federal crime, and the 1934 U.S. Congress gave special agents the authority to make arrests and carry firearms. After World War II, the FBI began conducting background security investigations for government agencies, as well as probes into internal security matters for the executive branch of the federal government. The 1960s brought civil rights and organized crime to the forefront for the FBI, and the '70s and '80s focused on counterterrorism, financial crime, drugs, and violent crimes. During the 1990s the FBI continued to focus on these crimes, as well as to address the growing threat of cybercrime. The bureau created the Computer Investigations and Infrastructure Threat Assessment Center and other initiatives to respond to physical and cyber attacks against infrastructure in the United States. The FBI's mission changed as a result of the terrorist attacks of September 11, 2001. While still investigating all types of federal crime, the bureau's most important mandate today is to protect the American people from future terrorist attacks.

may also have to work nights or go for extended periods of time with little or poor sleep. Another drawback to the job is, of course, the physical hazards it presents. Agents, depending on their assignment, may risk their lives while on the job, and some have died in the line of duty. Despite the long hours and sometimes extreme conditions, many agents find the job fun and intriguing. "Being an FBI agent is the best job in the world," John says. "It's always interesting, always challenging, rewarding, affords agents a lot of freedom to investigate cases as they see fit, and allows us to serve the taxpayers and benefit society. I am about seven years from mandatory retirement, and I have no intention of leaving any time before that."

Julia Meredith also works in the FBI's Chicago Division. She has been an FBI agent since 2001. She works on Squad WC-3 (White Collar #3), which investigates public corruption (corruption of judges, law enforcement officers, public employees, and politicians at the local, state, and federal level). "Probably the best experience I have had as an agent," she says, "was one of my first experiences—taking the oath. Swearing to support and defend the Constitution of the United States of America against all enemies foreign and domestic was an incredible moment in my life. The responsibility that is placed upon an agent by taking that oath is an awesome thing, one that I take very, very seriously."

Julia's work varies daily, which she says is one of the aspects of the job that she enjoys the most. "You will never be bored as an agent! There are some tedious duties, for example, reviewing bank documents produced pursuant to subpoena can be dull, but that is where you will often find the most important and valuable leads."

In addition to her regular duties, Julia is also a member of the Chicago Evidence Response Team (ERT), which, she says, "collects evidence from crime scenes as needed (think *CSI*). This is a collateral duty for me; not all agents are ERT members. I receive ERT refresher training on a quarterly basis also, on such topics as fingerprint identification and collection, blood spatter analysis, crime scene photography, etc. There is a two-week initial training for ERT, and members can choose to attend advanced training on other topics such as arson investigation or advanced fingerprint

To Be a Successful FBI Agent, You Should . . .

- be between the ages of 23 and 37 and a citizen of the United States or the Northern Mariana Islands

- be in excellent physical health

- have strong writing and speaking skills

- have the ability to use tact and good judgment, especially in challenging and quickly evolving situations

- be willing to relocate and be on call 24 hours a day

- enjoy meeting and dealing with people

retrieval techniques. Being a member of ERT definitely provides a different experience than routine casework for an agent—you never know when you'll be called out and what type of scene will be processed. It may be the locating and recovery of a buried body, a plane crash, a car fire, a multiple homicide."

DO I HAVE WHAT IT TAKES TO BE AN FBI AGENT?

To be an FBI agent, you must be at least 23, but not yet 37 years of age. You must be a citizen of the United States or the Northern Mariana Islands. Candidates must be available for assignment anywhere in the FBI's headquarters or field offices and possess a valid driver's license.

FBI agents must have the ability to use tact and good judgment, especially in challenging and quickly evolving situations. They need strong coping skills to deal with sudden events or crises. Agents must also have good observation skills and the ability to conduct an investigation in a discerning and efficient manner. They must be willing to relocate and be on call 24 hours a day, every day of the year—even when they are on vacation. "This job requires very long hours at times," says Julia Meredith. "Many interviews of witnesses are conducted in the evening, when most other people are home eating dinner. During a trial and the preparation leading to it, you will work seven days a week, an average of 14 hours a day. It can really consume your life, leaving little time for family and friends."

Since they work with different types of people every day, FBI agents should enjoy meeting and dealing with people. And it helps to have a broad knowledge of the world. For example, agents with art degrees have helped investigate international art theft rings. People who read a lot also make good agents, because they are curious and usually have more general knowledge. Agents also need to have good writing and speaking skills to carry them through court appearances.

FBI agents must be in excellent health to pass a physical exam. Applicants will be disqualified if they have a physical condition that interferes with firearm use, raids, or defensive tactics. If you are considering the job, you cannot be color blind, and you must have uncorrected vision of no less than 20/200 in each eye without glasses, corrected to 20/20 in one eye and no less than 20/40 in the other.

In addition, you may be disqualified if you have been convicted of a felony or major misdemeanor, have used illegal drugs, or fail to pass a polygraph test or drug test.

HOW DO I BECOME AN FBI AGENT?
Education

John Diwik says the he was always interested in the FBI—even back in elementary school. "I remember reading library books about the FBI when I was 9 or 10 years old," he says. John earned an undergraduate criminal justice degree from Northeastern University in Boston, Massachusetts. "After graduation," he says, "I applied to the bureau several times before I was accepted for employment. In fact, I went back to graduate school and obtained an MBA at the University of Connecticut before I was hired."

High School

A high school diploma, or its equivalent, is required. The FBI does not recommend specific courses for high school students. Rather, the bureau encourages students to do the best work they can. Since FBI agents perform a variety of work, numerous academic disciplines are needed. John offers the following advice to high school students who are interested in a career with the FBI: "Stay away from drugs and stay out of trouble. Get a college degree in an area that interests you, and strive for good grades. Stay physically fit and pursue hobbies and extracurricular activities. Upon graduation, and once you turn 23, apply to the FBI. Be persistent (I was) and you may be lucky enough to be selected."

Postsecondary Training

Candidates must be graduates from a four-year resident program at a college or university that is accredited by one of the regional or national institutional associations recognized by the U.S. Department of Education. No specific major is required of applicants. "The diversity of the backgrounds of FBI agents is what makes the FBI special," John says. "There are agents who can do anything and everything. We have chemists, engineers, lawyers, teachers, computer people, accountants, and language specialists, among others."

Regardless of the degree they earn, Julia Meredith recommends that students think twice about seeking employment with the FBI straight out of college. "The bureau does occasionally hire people a year or two out of college," she says, "but my experience has generally been that people who have a few years of professional experience bring more to the table as an agent. As an agent, you will draw more on your professional and personal experiences than you ever will on any degree."

The bureau offers entrance programs in law, accounting, language, and diversified studies. The law school program accepts law school graduates with two years of undergraduate work. The accounting school program accepts accounting graduates who have also passed the Uniform Certified Public Accountant Examination, or provided proof from their undergraduate school that they are academically eligible to sit for the exam. The language program accepts graduates who speak a foreign language fluently; the bureau has a current need for such agents. The diversified program accepts graduates who possess three years of full-time work experience, or an advanced degree and two years of work experience.

Applicants with law or accounting degrees are especially valued by the FBI. Since agents investigate violations of federal law, a law degree may give applicants an appreciation and understanding of the Federal Rules of Criminal Procedure. Plus, a law degree should help agents identify the elements of a criminal violation and collect the necessary evidence for successful prosecution. Since FBI agents trace financial transactions and review and analyze complex accounting records, an accounting degree will likely help agents document evidence and reveal sophisticated financial crimes.

FBI agent applicants are required to take a written exam. Those passing the exam will then be interviewed based on their overall qualifications and the needs of the bureau. Applicants being considered for employment must undergo a thorough background investigation, a polygraph test, and a urinalysis to determine illegal drug usage.

If appointed to the position of an FBI special agent, new hires train for 18 weeks at the FBI Academy in Quantico, Virginia. Agent trainees spend a total of 708 instructional hours studying academic and investigative subjects, and trainees also focus on physical fitness, defensive tactics, and firearms training. Emphasis is placed on developing investigative techniques, as well as skills in interviewing, interrogation, and gathering intelligence information. Agent trainees are tested on their defensive tactics, firearms and weapon handling, physical fitness, and arrest techniques. They must also pass academic exams and obey certain rules and regulations during the training. If the trainees pass the tests at the academy and receive their credentials, they become special agents and are assigned to serve a two-year probationary period at an FBI field office.

Internships and Volunteership

Each summer the FBI offers the Honors Internship Program to a select group of outstanding undergraduate and graduate

> ## Advancement Possibilities
>
> *Assistant special agents in charge* supervise specific programs— such as those designed to deal with financial crime and domestic terrorism—and special agents.
>
> *Special agents in charge* oversee a field office or program area, report to the FBI headquarters, and are usually in charge of at least 100 people.
>
> *Supervisory special agents* are supervisors of a squad who ensure that all procedures are complied with and that the squad has everything they need to conduct their job. (A squad includes the agents and sometimes support employees needed to work a specific violation.)

students. The program allows qualified participants to spend the summer working for the FBI in Washington, D.C., and learn about the bureau's operations and career opportunities. The program is extremely competitive and selects only individuals with strong academic credentials, outstanding character, a high degree of motivation, and the ability to represent the FBI upon return to their campus.

To be considered, undergraduate candidates must be enrolled in their junior or senior years when they apply to the program, and graduate students must be enrolled full time at a college or university. Applicants must have a cumulative grade point average of at least 3.0 (on a scale of 4.0) and be returning to their campus after the program. All candidates must be U.S. citizens.

To apply for the program, contact the FBI field office closest to your campus for an application. You must complete and return an FD-646a application form, current academic transcript, résumé, recent photograph, written recommendation from the appropriate dean or department head, and a 500-word essay expressing your interest in the program. Application packages should be submitted before November 1.

Qualified candidates are interviewed and each field office nominates candidates to the FBI Personnel Division by December 1. A headquarters selection committee chooses the finalists, who must then pass an extensive background investigation and drug-screening test. The director of the FBI gives final approval for program participants. Selections are based on academic achievement, area of study, life or work experiences, and interest in law enforcement. Because of the bureau's long-term needs, students with skills and education in the areas of engineering, computer science, foreign languages, political science, law, accounting, and the physical sciences receive special consideration.

Once selected, FBI interns are assigned to a headquarters division based on their academic discipline, their potential contribution to the division, and the needs of the FBI. Interns work side by side with FBI agents and learn about the inner operations of the bureau. Undergraduate interns are paid at the government's GS-6 grade level—about $27,507 annually in

2004—and graduate interns are paid at the GS-7 level—about $30,567 annually in 2004. Interns' travel expenses to and from the Washington, D.C., program are reimbursed by the FBI.

In addition to the Honors Internship Program, the FBI offers several other internship opportunities. Visit https://www.fbijobs.gov/231.asp for more information.

If you are interested in a career with the FBI, you may apply for internships, volunteer opportunities, and other programs offered through your local police departments, which will give you experience and insight into aspects of law enforcement in general.

WHO WILL HIRE ME?

The FBI employed 12,617 special agents as of August 31, 2006. The FBI hires on a continual basis, although some years it does not hire any new agents. When the bureau is hiring, they advertise in newspapers, internal postings, and on the Internet.

If you are interested in working for the FBI, contact the applicant coordinator at the FBI field office nearest you or visit the FBI's job Web site, https://www.fbijobs.gov. The bureau will send you information on existing vacancies, requirements for the positions, how to file applications, and locations where examinations will be given.

Julia Meredith decided to become an agent because she saw an ad in the newspaper. "Pretty mundane, I know!" she recalls. "There is some back story to it, though. One of my first jobs out of college was as an air quality inspector for a state environmental protection agency. (I have a bachelor's degree in environmental science with a minor in biology.) I really enjoyed the investigatory aspects of the job. I left that job in 1994 to work for a chemical company as an environmental manager for one of their manufacturing plants. In 1999, my responsibilities included a position as industry representative on the local emergency planning commission (LEPC). As an LEPC member, I attended a conference on domestic terrorism (DT), where I saw a presentation by several agents about the FBI's response to the Oklahoma City (1995) and World Trade Center (1993) bombings. I was so impressed by the professionalism and knowledge of the agents and the work the bureau had done, I thought 'I would love to be a part of that organization.' However, at that time I was under the impression that agents had to be attorneys or accountants, or have prior military or police experience, none of which applied to me. Not long after the DT conference, I saw an ad in the paper, listing the minimum qualifications for agents, and realized that I did qualify. I sent in the initial application, and lo and behold, 22 months and many more applications and tests later, I went to Quantico for training."

Other Career Opportunities in the FBI

Besides the special agent position, the FBI hires people for jobs listed in four categories: professional, administrative, technical, and clerical. Professional positions include attorneys, chemists, personnel psychologists, and contract specialists. Administrative positions include intelligence research specialists, computer specialists, management analysts, and language specialists. Technical positions include evidence technicians, accounting technicians, and computer operators. Clerical positions include secretaries, personnel assistants, office automation assistants, and file clerks.

WHERE CAN I GO FROM HERE?

FBI promotions are awarded mainly on performance, rather than seniority. All administrative and supervisory jobs are filled from within the ranks by agents who have demonstrated their ability to handle more responsibility. Some FBI agents climb the ladder to become higher-grade administrators and supervisors. For example, an agent may become an inspector, supervisory special agent, or special agent in charge of a field office. Agents may also be assigned to the FBI headquarters, or they may become headquarters supervisors, unit and section chiefs, and division heads. Agents may retire after 20 years of service, and after the age of 50; mandatory retirement is required at the age of 57. In some instances, agents may be granted one-year extensions up until the age of 60.

John Diwik would like to assume a supervisory special agent position within the FBI in the next several years. "I would like to work several years as a supervisor before I retire." Retired FBI agents often become consultants, teachers, attorneys, and private investigators. Many retirees also work for security departments of large corporations. "After the FBI," John says, "I am planning on a second career in corporate America. With my experience and educational background, I anticipate that I will be able to find a lucrative position in the private sector."

"I would like to continue to be the best case agent I can be in the next 5 or 10 years," Julia Meredith says. "I really enjoy working cases and love my job. I'm not going anywhere!"

> ### Related Jobs
>
> - air marshals
> - border patrol agents
> - deputy sheriffs
> - detectives
> - fingerprint classifiers
> - fire investigators
> - fish and game wardens
> - forensic experts
> - narcotics investigators
> - police officers
> - private investigators
> - state highway patrol officers
> - U.S. marshals

WHAT ARE THE SALARY RANGES?

New FBI agents start out at the federal government's GS-10 level—approximately $41,175 in 2005, depending on where the agent lives. Salaries for agents are increased slightly if they reside in cities such as New York, Los Angeles, and Miami that have a high cost of living. Agents also receive an additional 25 percent of their base pay (known as availability pay) as compensation for being available 24 hours a day, seven days a week. FBI agents can earn within-grade pay increases upon satisfactory job performance, and grade increases may be earned as the agent gains experience through good job performance. FBI agents in nonsupervisory positions can reach the GS-13 grade—about $64,478 in 2005. Agents who move into management positions can earn a GS-15 salary—about $89,625. Some agents then move into a different employment category called the Senior Executive Service, where they make more than $100,000 annually working for the FBI. Benefits include paid vacation, health and life insurance, retirement, sick leave, and job-related tuition reimbursement.

WHAT IS THE JOB OUTLOOK?

Most job vacancies within the FBI are expected as agents retire, advance, or resign. Turnover has traditionally been low, as most agents remain with the FBI until the age of mandatory retirement.

The numbers of FBI special agents are linked to the scope of the FBI's responsibilities. Increases in organized crimes, white-collar crimes, and terrorist threats on American soil have led the FBI to increase the number of agents in recent years.

As the bureau's responsibilities expand, it will create new positions to meet them. Despite increased recruitment, growth in the numbers of new agency hires is expected to remain somewhat limited. Competition for openings will continue to be extremely high. According to the *Chicago Tribune*, the typical recruit is between the ages of 27 and 31, has a graduate-level education, and is physically fit. Since the terrorist attacks, the FBI is particularly interested in recruits who are able to speak Arabic and are familiar with Middle and Far Eastern culture. Potential agents with backgrounds in information technology are also in high demand.

Federal Aviation Security Workers

SUMMARY

Definition
Federal aviation security worker is a blanket term describing people in several jobs—such as security screeners and air marshals—who protect the safety of passengers and staff in the nation's airports and aircraft.

Alternative Job Titles
Air marshals
Aviation security directors

Baggage and passenger screeners
Security screeners

Salary Range
$23,000 to $35,000 to $150,000+

Educational Requirements
Some postsecondary training

Certification or Licensing
None available

Employment Outlook
Faster than the average

High School Subjects
Computer science
Government
Law
Mathematics
Physical education

Personal Interests
Airplanes
Current events
Exercise/personal fitness
Helping people: protection
Law
Psychology
Travel

Protecting U.S. skies, airports, and passengers is a huge undertaking that requires many qualified, well-trained individuals in different security roles. "Work as a screener is a challenging career," says Kelly Martin, who has worked as a security screener for three years. "The best part of my day is when passengers tell me how much they appreciate what I do for them and their families."

WHAT DOES A FEDERAL AVIATION SECURITY WORKER DO?

The most visible federal aviation security worker is the *security screener*, also called the *baggage and passenger screener*. These workers are responsible for identifying dangerous objects or hazardous materials in baggage, in cargo, or on traveling passengers and for preventing these objects and their carriers from boarding planes. They use computers, X-ray machines, and handheld scanners to screen bags and their owners passing through airport terminals. In addition to using technology to help them identify dangerous items, they also have to depend on their own eyesight to catch suspicious behavior and read the X-ray screens for signs of danger. These workers must be focused and alert, while also remaining personable and courteous to people being screened. The screening process can take a lot of time during high-volume travel days, and passengers waiting in line may be late for a flight, impatient, or simply rude. For this reason, security screeners must be people oriented, able to manage crowds, and able to maintain composure in stressful conditions.

The need for security is not limited to the ground. *Air marshals* have the demanding job of protecting all airline passengers and staff from onboard threats, such as terrorists, hijackers, bombs, or other weapons. These workers are often covert in their operations, meaning they may be dressed and seated like an average passenger, in order to watch for suspicious behavior and surprise a potential attacker. Many details of air marshal jobs are classified to protect national security, such as their exact number and identities, routes, and training procedures. However, their job is much like the work of a Secret Service agent. They must be attentive to all activity that goes on around them, identify potential threats to security, and deal with dangerous individuals

or objects once exposed on board. The main difference between air marshals and other types of federal aviation security workers is that they must be trained and able to handle possible warfare in a confined space at 30,000 feet in the air.

Another federal aviation security job of high importance is that of *aviation security director*. These workers, hired by the federal government, are responsible for all security personnel within an airport. They oversee the hiring, training, and work of baggage and passenger screeners and other security guards. In the nation's largest airports, such as LaGuardia in New York City or O'Hare in Chicago, directors are in charge of hundreds of workers. Because of the high level of responsibility held in such a role, aviation security directors often have previous experience in crisis management or law enforcement, in positions such as police chief and military officer.

WHAT IS IT LIKE TO BE A FEDERAL AVIATION SECURITY WORKER?

David Smith has been a security screener at Chicago's O'Hare International Airport for three years. "There are many reasons why I decided to work with the Transportation Security Administration [the government agency that employs all security screeners]," he says. "First, I wanted to make a difference due to the aftermath of 9/11, and this job gave me that opportunity. Secondly, I majored in travel and airline management in college and wanted to utilize my industry expertise in my current job. Finally, I wanted to take a position where I could set a career path."

David works with the Response Team. "We are a hardworking and dedicated crew of screeners who perform security operations throughout the airport in areas where there is high passenger or baggage volume—where we are needed most. The greatest aspect of being part of this team is moving from one area to the next. Never being in one place for more than a few hours gives me the chance to meet and work with new people all the time. My responsibilities as a lead screener on the Response Team include interacting with the screening managers to determine where the greatest need is in order to dispatch the screener workforce. I also assist in giving weekly train-

To Be a Successful Security Screener, You Should . . .

- be able to stay calm under pressure
- be able to stand for hours at a time
- have the physical strength to lift passengers' luggage
- have a keen eye for detail
- have strong communication skills
- have excellent vision, hearing, and manual dexterity

ing classes and oversee the screener and supervisor relationship."

Kelly Martin has also worked as a security screener at O'Hare International Airport for three years. "I entered this career because I love to work with people," he says. "I enjoy keeping busy, and I love a challenge. This career has it all."

Kelly starts his day by attending a daily briefing. "Then," he says, "we are assigned to a terminal and/or checkpoint. As a checkpoint screener, my main duties are ensuring the safety of the traveling public by performing screening at the airport checkpoint and providing customer service. For this job, one needs to be alert and ready to work. I operate an X-ray machine, stand at the walk-thru metal detector, instruct people what to do before entering the sterile area, check bags when needed, and explain to people what options they have if they have a

To Be a Successful Air Marshal, You Should . . .

- have a calm demeanor when under pressure
- be in good physical shape to face and dominate potential attackers
- have excellent vision and hearing
- have a keen eye for detail
- be willing to spend a considerable amount of time away from home
- be willing to work at all hours of the day

prohibited item. I properly dispose of prohibited items that people surrender."

DO I HAVE WHAT IT TAKES TO BE A FEDERAL AVIATION SECURITY WORKER?

All federal aviation security personnel have demanding jobs that require a calm demeanor when under pressure. Screeners often have to stand for hours at a time and assist in lifting passengers' luggage onto the screening belt. "I like this job but one has to be very careful to not get injured," David Smith says. "Physical labor involving lifting of travelers' bags can take a toll on the body if one doesn't do it properly." Screeners' eyesight must be strong enough to detect even the smallest of possible threats displayed on a computer screen. To ensure that individuals can handle these demands, potential screeners face many physical and vision

tests to ensure they are up to the job. As of November 2001, all screeners must be U.S. citizens or nationals and pass tests evaluating mental abilities (English reading, writing, and speaking), visual observation (including color perception), hearing, and manual dexterity. Similarly, air marshals must pass vision and hearing tests and be in good physical shape to face and dominate potential attackers.

The job of air marshals can be extremely stressful. These workers must be prepared to overcome an attacker (who may be ready to die for his or her cause), all in a confined space without risking harm to any of the plane's passengers. In addition, air marshals must spend considerable time away from home.

Aviation security directors must have strong management and communication skills. They must have an analytical mind and a comprehensive knowledge of security procedures and practices.

HOW DO I BECOME A FEDERAL AVIATION SECURITY WORKER?
Education
High School

To work in most federal aviation security jobs, you should have at least a high school diploma. However, security screeners can sidestep this educational requirement with previous job experience in security. While in high school, take classes in history and government to familiarize yourself with historical events and current threats to our national security, such as

A Short History of Airport Security

The use of screening and onboard security personnel is not a recent invention. The presence of guards on airplanes originated in the 1960s as a result of a number of hijackings of U.S. planes flying to and from Cuba. These guards, referred to as sky marshals, grew in number during the 1970s, then declined in later years with the lower occurrences of airplane hijackings. Airplane security staffing reached several thousand workers at the peak of this hijacking scare, but then dropped to fewer than 100 workers nationwide during its quietest times.

The 2001 terrorist attacks on the World Trade Center and the Pentagon spurred many changes in the realm of airport security. Under President George W. Bush's administration, a new federal agency was born: the Transportation Security Administration, responsible for overseeing all security at the nation's airports. This agency made airport and airline security a federal responsibility, and as a result, all airport security personnel became federal employees. This was no small task. Previously, security screening in airports was handled by private security firms. These firms were inconsistent in their hiring and training methods and paid relatively low wages—resulting in high job turnover rates and inadequate screening of potentially dangerous objects and materials. With the shift of responsibility into the government's hands, standard training and hiring requirements were put in place. In addition to better screening, hiring, and training methods, the technology for screening bags and passengers has improved, increasing the chances that dangerous cargo and on-person threats can be located and prevented from boarding a plane.

foreign hijackers and terrorist operations. You should also be comfortable working with computers since most jobs in security involve a great deal of technology. Math classes can be beneficial because, as a security worker, you must be analytical and observant to identify and catch dangers before they happen. If you plan to become an air marshal, take as many physical education classes as you can. It is also a good idea to take government, history, criminal justice, and psychology classes. Aspiring security directors should take computer science, government, history, criminal justice, law, mathematics, and psychology classes.

Postsecondary Training

Screeners and air marshals are highly trained before starting their jobs. Screeners learn how to operate and identify dangerous objects from the X-ray machines and handheld wands. They also must be prepared to manage potentially dangerous individuals. Screeners currently receive 40 hours of training before their first day at work, and receive an additional 60 hours of training while on the job. This training period may be extended due to increased scrutiny on screeners' performance and heightened national security risks.

Air marshals are rigorously trained in classified training centers across the country, and come to the job with previous on-the-job experience from serving in a military or civilian police force.

Aviation security directors do not receive much on-the-job training because these individuals are already at the top of their profession and have years of training and experience in the field when they are hired.

Internships and Volunteerships

Due to the classified nature of these careers, there is little opportunity to participate in an internship directly with the Transportation Security Administration. Your college may offer internships with other law enforcement agencies that will give you a general idea of the daily lives of law enforcement officers.

Consider volunteering with your local police department or other law enforcement agency. While you won't get to chase criminals, you will get to work closely with law enforcement officers and to ask them questions about their careers.

WHO WILL HIRE ME?

In late 2001, airport and airline security was placed under the oversight of the federal government. While some screening jobs may still be handled by private companies, all security personnel are now screened and trained under federal rules

and regulations. This shift in responsibility was implemented to improve standards in security and ensure the safety of U.S. passengers and airline staff. The newly created Transportation Security Administration employs all security screeners, air marshals, and aviation security directors. There are approximately 43,000 security screeners working in the nation's airports; the number of air marshals and aviation security directors is classified.

Depending on the security level at which you want to be employed, you can start out working with no more than a high school diploma and on-the-job training. Security screening jobs are a great way to start out in this line of work. These jobs provide frontline experience in airport security, and can offer flexible part-time schedules.

Positions as air marshals or directors of security are not entry-level positions. If you are interested in one of these jobs, you will need previous employment experience in the police force, the U.S. military, or another position in which you have gained skills in protecting the lives of others.

WHERE CAN I GO FROM HERE?

Screening jobs have high turnover rates, and as a result, offer many chances for advancement. After a couple of years of experience in baggage and passenger screening, you can work your way into higher positions—in management or with busier traffic responsibility. Aviation security directors may be responsible for hundreds of workers and oversee the hiring and training of new workers.

Positions as air marshals already offer a high level of responsibility, but qualified and talented individuals can advance into roles as managers and directors, responsible for hundreds and even thousands of workers.

WHAT ARE THE SALARY RANGES?

Before the Transportation Security Administration was created to oversee airline security, screeners were paid minimum wage. In order to attract and retain qualified and dedicated workers, earnings have improved considerably, with most full-time screeners earning salaries of $23,000 to $35,000 a year. Their pay increases as their level of experience and responsibility increases. Air marshals and directors earn much more; aviation security directors pull in salaries of $150,000 or more—making them among the highest-paid employees in government service.

WHAT IS THE JOB OUTLOOK?

With the new awareness of airline dangers following the 2001 terrorist attacks, the employment of aviation security workers will grow at a faster-than-average rate. Despite better pay, security screeners still have high turnover rates due to the demands of the job. This turnover will continue to create many new jobs in the future. While jobs as air marshals and aviation security directors will not be as plentiful, there will always be a critical need for qualified and skilled individuals to protect airplanes and passengers from security threats.

Firefighters

SUMMARY

Definition
Professional firefighters serve the public by protecting citizens and their property from fire and its effects. Firefighters also respond to other types of emergencies, including emergency medical incidents, hazardous material spills, and various types of rescue calls.

Alternative Job Titles
Smoke jumpers
Wildland firefighters

Salary Range
$20,000 to $38,000 to $60,000+

Educational Requirements
High school diploma

Certification or Licensing
Required

Employment Outlook
Faster than the average

High School Subjects
Computer science
Health
Physical education

Personal Interests
Helping people: physical health/medicine
Helping people: protection

It's about 10:00 A.M. on a sunny August day when the call comes in: Smoke and flames are pouring out of a large apartment complex. The firefighters quickly don their heavy, fire-resistant bunkers, jump onto the fire engines, and head downtown. Captain John DeJulio leads them.

John's adrenaline pumps as he arrives on the scene, less than two minutes after the call came in. Heavy, black smoke rushes out of a third-story window. People lean out the windows yelling for help.

Two firefighters grab a heavy fire hose and drag it up the stairs to the burning third-story apartment. The carpet is already melting from the intense heat in the room. Some firefighters hoist ladders to rescue the people hanging from the windows. John and several other firefighters connect their masks to their air tanks and run into the building to get people out. Smoke fills the corridors, which have already heated to about 200 degrees near the floor and even hotter near the ceiling. A tenant in his 60s, who is trying to put out the fire with a fire extinguisher, is overcome by smoke. The firefighters rescue him from the building and perform CPR until the man is taken to the hospital.

Lingo to Learn

fire point The temperature at which a flammable liquid emits enough vapors to sustain a fire ignited by an outside source.

flash over The temperature at which everything in a room reaches ignition temperature and spontaneously ignites.

flash point The temperature at which a flammable liquid emits enough vapors to briefly ignite when an outside ignition source is present.

ignition temperature The temperature at which a substance ignites without an outside ignition source.

water hammer The potentially damaging surge of water that results when the flow of water though a fire hose or pipe is suddenly stopped. Can often be heard as a distinct, sharp clank.

The crew is able to contain and extinguish the fire fairly quickly, but the man dies. Then the firefighters begin the laborious job of removing the charred debris. Later they learn that the fire was started by a five-year-old playing with matches.

WHAT DOES A FIREFIGHTER DO?

Professional firefighters must be ready in seconds to jump on a fire engine, drive to a fire, and then work to protect and rescue people, extinguish the fire, and save personal property. While firefighting can be rewarding, it is one of the most dangerous professions. Nearly 40 percent of all professional firefighters are injured every year. Every day firefighters risk their lives by responding to fire calls, as well as emergency medical requests, hazardous material spills, and various types of rescue calls. Besides the danger of fire, firefighters may jeopardize their own safety through exposure to toxic materials and contagious diseases such as tuberculosis, hepatitis, and HIV.

During fire suppression calls, firefighters are required to connect hose lines to hydrants, operate pumps, apply water or other extinguishing agents through hose lines and nozzles, and position ladders. Firefighters also ventilate smoke-filled areas, operate heavy equipment, salvage building contents, rescue victims, and administer emergency medical care. After the fire is extinguished, firefighters remove the debris (they call it "overhaul") and often remain at the scene to ensure that the fire does not start again.

When responding to a fire call, firefighters wear protective gear to prevent their hands and bodies from being burned. They may also use a self-contained breathing apparatus. Once the fire is extinguished, fire investigators or fire marshals may examine the site to determine the cause of the fire, especially if they suspect the fire was set intentionally, or if it resulted in injury or death.

Besides responding to fire suppression calls, most professional firefighters are trained as emergency medical technicians or paramedics to provide emergency medical care to ill or injured people. Firefighters carry equipment such as cardiac defibrillators and life-saving medication, and they are trained to stabilize and transport sick or hurt people to hospitals.

Responding to fires and emergency medical calls are the most visible aspects of working as a firefighter, but the job entails other duties as well. Firefighters are also responsible for dealing with incident command, hazardous materials, high angle rescue, water and ice rescue, wildland fires, fire prevention, fire investigations, communications, fire education, and community relations. In addition, they may be required to respond to environmental emergencies such as earthquakes, floods, and blizzards. Most professional firefighters educate the people in their community on the hazards of fire, and teach school children about the dangers of fire and the correct reactions to emergency situations.

In addition, some firefighters are trained to prevent fires by inspecting buildings for trash, chemicals, and hazardous conditions that may result in a fire. *Inspectors* check exit routes, oversee the storage and use of flammable and combustible materials, supervise the occupancy limits of public places, and monitor the use of equipment or materials in all types of buildings to ensure that local fire and building codes are being met and that hazardous conditions are not present. Faulty or damaged wiring and inadequate alarm systems may also pose fire hazards. Substandard conditions are reported to the property owner, who is legally bound to correct them. Fire inspectors may also present fire prevention programs to local school and civic groups.

When firefighters are not on a call or dealing with the public, they clean and maintain their equipment to keep it immaculate. Mechanical equipment is polished and lubricated, water hoses are washed, and personal protective gear is kept in excellent condition. Firefighters also attend training courses and conduct practice drills to improve their skills and knowledge of firefighting and emergency medical techniques. Downtime is often spent studying for examinations, which usually influence firefighters' opportunities for promotion. Many firefighters read professional journals to keep abreast of technological developments and administrative practices and procedures.

Since many firefighters live at the fire station during their shift—for up to 24 hours at a time—those on duty perform housekeeping and cleaning duties. Chores include cooking meals, cleaning bathrooms, and making beds. Many fire stations offer exercise facilities, which are available to help firefighters increase and maintain their physical abilities.

While the vast majority of professional firefighters work for municipal fire departments, industrial plants also hire professional firefighters to prevent and suppress fires. In addition, airports hire firefighters to prevent and combat fires and save passengers and crew members in the event of a crash or accident. Other professionals work for the federal or state government as *wildland firefighters*, often parachuting out of airplanes to get to inaccessible forest fires. These parachuting firefighters are often called *smoke jumpers.*

WHAT IS IT LIKE TO BE A FIREFIGHTER?

John DeJulio has been a firefighter since he was 17 years old. "I grew up in the town of Colonie in upstate New York," he says. "The town is covered by 12 volunteer firefighting departments. Firefighting was a family tradition, as my father was past chief at one of the volunteer departments, and my mom used to ride the ambulance. The volunteer department provided a number of social activities as well—such as firefighter competitions and stock fire truck racing. It didn't take long for me to discover that this was a rewarding career.

Did You Know?

The first permanent firefighting company was formed in Philadelphia in 1736 by Benjamin Franklin, followed by New York in 1737, and then the remaining colonies. Population growth during the nineteenth century led to an increased need for professional firefighters and proper equipment, and many cities suffered devastating fires as a result of an insufficient water supply, crowded conditions, and poor building techniques. In 1871, the Great Chicago Fire killed 250 people, destroyed practically all of the city, and caused $196 million in property losses. Fire prevention week, scheduled in October of each year, commemorates the Great Chicago Fire.

It is a noble profession, as well—something that the community admires."

In time, John became an officer with the Fuller Road Fire Department and, in 1980, volunteered to serve as a firefighter at the Winter Olympics in Lake Placid, New York. He moved to Olathe, Kansas, in 1991 to become a paid firefighter, and is now a captain with the Olathe Fire Department in Olathe, Kansas.

John's primary goals as a fire captain are to protect people, save property, and ease the pain and suffering that result from emergency situations such as fires, car accidents, chemical spills, and natural disasters. John works 24-hour shifts, starting at 8:00 A.M. "When you first arrive at the station (making sure you get there about 15 minutes early)," he explains, "you meet with the captain who is going off duty to discuss what they did the prior shift (i.e., the equipment used and any updates or information that needs to be passed on). Then you put your firefighting gear on the truck and check your air pack (by placing your face in the mask and turning on the bottle, looking it over to make sure that it is working properly and the bottle is full). I then go to my office and look at the daily activity calendar to see if I have any public relations events, meetings, or training scheduled. I then review the schedule with the crew so they can plan their daily duties. I then go back to the office and print out the day's shift schedule, which indicates the location of each firefighter and the station he/she is working at. This is also the time that I open and read my e-mails and other correspondence. I then check the status of the crew members and their daily duties. If they need help, I chip in and help."

From 9:00 to noon, John and his fellow firefighters participate in training or meetings. Of course, all preplanned activities stop as emergency calls come in. Firefighters must be ready to drop whatever they are doing to respond to calls. "On a typical day," John says, "we answer 10 to 15 emergency calls, which, in most cities, would make our station one of the busier stations." After a break for lunch, John and his team continue to respond to calls and participate in community outreach programs such as an adopt-a-school program; this is a program, John explains, "that teaches local third graders about fire safety and other related dangers (bicycle safety, first aid, and severe weather)."

Around 4:00 P.M., John and his fellow firefighters try to do some physical activity, whether lifting weights or running on a treadmill. Being in top physical shape allows firefighters to be at their best when responding to dangerous situations. After a break for dinner, the firefighters might tackle committee work or schoolwork that needs to be completed. "This is also considered downtime when family members can visit and you can watch television and relax," John explains. "Around 8:00 P.M. is when the bunk (or your bed) has to be made for the night. Firefighters can retire for the night anytime after 8:00; but usually we sit around and watch television and play

cards until 11:00 or 11:30 P.M. We usually receive two or three emergency calls during the night." Whether they have had a good night of sleep or not, John and his crew must wake up at 7:00 A.M. and prepare the equipment and fire truck for the incoming crew.

In addition to responding to emergency calls, John has other duties. "When you return to the firehouse after each call," John explains, "a report has to be completed on the computer, either by the paramedic for any medical call or by the captain (me) for all other calls. The report usually takes about 10 to 15 minutes to complete. As captain, I also serve as the station resource officer for building and appliance repairs and other general maintenance; if something breaks, I have to file a report. In addition, each captain is assigned a project to oversee; mine is firefighting gear. I am responsible for ordering new gear, sending things out for repair, and inspecting gear on a routine basis."

Depending on local conditions, professional firefighters work between 40 and 56 hours a week. To ensure that crews are available at all hours of the day, professional firefighters work in shifts—most often the 24-hour tour or the split shift. The 24-hour shift requires firefighters to work 24 hours on duty followed by either 48 or 72 hours off. The split shift requires firefighters to work either nine-hour days and 15-hour nights, or 10-hour days and 14-hour nights. After each set of day shifts, a firefighter receives about 72 hours off, and after each set of night shifts, a fire-

To Be a Successful Firefighter, You Should . . .

- be committed to protecting and saving lives and property
- have courage, confidence, physical agility, and endurance
- be able to make quick decisions in emergencies
- be able to get along well with others and be comfortable working as a member of a team
- have good communication skills
- be able to deal with tragedy and death

fighter is given 48 hours off. "I always joke that the best part of the job is that I only work 10 days a month," John says. "People hear that and forget that those 10 days are 24-hour shifts, which is equivalent to a 56-hour workweek! However, this schedule leaves more time for my family and hobbies."

Whatever the shift, the work of a firefighter can be extremely dangerous. According to the U.S. Fire Administration, more than 100 firefighters die in service to their communities each year, and about 100,000 suffer injuries, many of which are very serious. Firefighters work in all kinds of weather and conditions, often battling heat, flames, smoke, gases, chemicals, and poisonous fumes; and facing the risk of building collapse.

DO I HAVE I WHAT IT TAKES TO BE A FIREFIGHTER?

Above all, firefighters must be committed to their job of protecting and saving lives and property. Without that commitment, the dangerous conditions and long hours turn many people away from this career. Firefighters should possess courage, confidence, knowledge, physical agility, and endurance, but they also need compassion and adaptability to be successful. "Firefighters have to be quick thinkers and reactors," John says. "You also need have to have common sense. You need to treat every patient as if he or she was one of your own family."

Firefighters must make quick decisions in emergencies, so initiative and good judgment are important. Because firefighters eat, sleep, and work closely together under stressful and dangerous conditions, they should also be reliable, able to get along well with others, and comfortable working with a team. Leadership qualities are vital for officers, who direct the activities of fire fighting crews, and establish and maintain discipline and efficient operations.

Good communication skills are also vital to the field. Firefighters need to find out pertinent information from different types of people ranging from an elderly fire victim to a toddler injured in a car accident. Another important characteristic for firefighters is the ability to accept that they will be away from their families during critical times. "You never know when, where, or what the next emergency is going to be," John says. "During times of severe weather or terrorist attacks, we can't be home with our families; sometimes not knowing how they are after such an event is stressful."

Firefighters must stay up to date regarding new techniques and advancements in firefighting. "Firefighters," says John, "must always be willing to learn new tactics and procedures as they are developed and changed within the fire service."

HOW DO I BECOME A FIREFIGHTER?

Education

John looks back at his work as a volunteer firefighter in upstate New York as the jumpstart to his career. "Most people either enter the fire service through the military or start with no experience at all," he explains. "I was able to attend classes and obtain certificates for pump and ladder operations, as well as haz-mat response, EMT, and Firefighter 1 and 2. This was a tremendous help when I applied for the Olathe Fire Department, as I already had the training and experience necessary."

High School

Virtually every fire department requires applicants to possess a high school diploma or its equivalent. Classes pertaining to human anatomy, physics, and chemistry are helpful, and you should also learn about computers, which are becoming more and more useful for fire departments. Some departments are already relying on computerized systems to help them determine the best route to a fire. Some fire departments use the Internet to collect a variety of information on topics ranging from the weather to other departments' procedures. In the future, computer simulations may show firefighters the best method to extinguish specific fires.

Considering the wide variety of tasks firefighters perform, most high school classes are beneficial. For example, auto shop could help firefighters maintain fire trucks, family and consumer sciences would help with meal preparation, and theater or drama classes may help with public fire education presentations, such as puppet shows.

Postsecondary Training

Generally people become professional firefighters between the ages of 18 and 35. Most fire departments require applicants to be U.S. citizens and have a driver's license; some departments require candidates to be residents of the community in which they intend to serve.

Applicants for most municipal firefighting jobs are required to take written and physical examinations. Candidates who pass those exams are usually interviewed and then ranked according to their scores. Then, when an opening comes up at a fire department, the applicants with the best test scores usually have the best chance of getting hired.

Applicants must also meet height and weight requirements. A drug test and security background check may be required, as well as a preexisting medical conditions exam and psychological screening.

Although it is not required, a growing number of candidates have a two- or four-year college degree when they apply for a fire-fighting job. John has an associate's degree in fire science. His employer, the Olathe Fire Department, provided him with tuition assistance. "An associate's degree is a requirement for anyone who wishes to promote to a captain's position," John explains. "Those who wish to continue to the rank of battalion chief and above must have a bachelor's degree, and must complete the Executive Fire Officer Program (http://www.usfa.dhs.gov/training/nfa/efop) at the National Fire Academy in Emmitsburg, Maryland."

Some departments require applicants to attend a firefighting training program at a vo-tech school or a two-year college degree program that teaches fire protection and control. In addition, some applicants are required to become certified emergency medical technicians or to receive hazardous materials training, and military applicants may be required to show they have been trained in firefighting techniques.

Firefighting testing is extremely rigorous and competitive. On average, it can take five years or more to get hired on a full-time permanent basis. For each position available, there are generally between 1,000 and 3,000 applicants.

Certification or Licensing

Professional firefighters are certified for firefighting according to standards established by their municipalities. Generally, new hires in large fire departments train for several weeks at their department's training center. New firefighters are taught in classrooms and in the field, and study

Advancement Possibilities

Captains are working supervisors in charge of the technical duties of a firefighting crew on an engine.

Battalion chiefs oversee captains on major incidents and develop specific strategies to deal with emergency calls.

Fire inspectors and investigators work to prevent fires by conducting inspections, public education efforts, and investigations.

the fundamentals of firefighting, fire prevention, ventilation, local building codes, hazardous materials, first aid, the use and care of equipment, and search-and-rescue techniques. They learn how to use axes, saws, chemical extinguishers, ladders, and other firefighting and rescue equipment.

Applicants in some small towns and communities may enter the profession through on-the-job training as volunteer firefighters, or by direct application to the local government. Once assigned to a fire department, professional firefighters usually serve a probationary period ranging from six months to one year. During this time, successful firefighters continue a rigorous training program and are then certified.

Internships and Volunteerships

If you attend a college program in firefighting, you will probably be required to participate in an internship. This hands-on experience will allow you to work closely with firefighters and other professionals. Contact the college that you plan to attend for more information on internships that might be available.

Labor Unions

Most career firefighters, especially those in larger cities, are union members. When a person becomes a professional firefighter, he or she has the opportunity to join the International Association of Firefighters (http://www.iaff.org/). This organization was formed in 1918 and strives to promote the welfare of its more than 267,000 members.

Another organization called the International Association of Arson Investigators (http://www.firearson.com) works to increase the knowledge and skills of professionals who investigate fires, explosions, and related catastrophes.

WHO WILL HIRE ME?

Most professional firefighters work for a municipal fire department, although some are employed with fire departments on federal and state installations, such as airports, and some serve as wildland firefighters. A small number of professional firefighters work for private companies. Contact these companies directly to inquire about firefighting positions.

To become a firefighter, you must first test with the hiring department and score high enough to make the "cut" list. Notices of these tests are often listed in newspaper classified advertisements, local job service agencies, or on bulletin boards in public buildings such as post offices and courthouses. The process can be time consuming and expensive. Graduates of two- or four-year firefighting or fire protection programs can get help from their school's career services office. Applicants may also write or call organizations to inquire about their testing dates and procedures.

Some prospective firefighters also pay to become members of subscription services, which forward department testing dates as they became available. Several sites on the Internet and telephone hotlines list testing information as well.

It is important to note that getting into the fire service is not an easy task. "It took many tries/applications/interviews and traveling to different parts of the country before I was successful in landing a position with a paid fire department," John recalls. "Some areas have civil service exams, some have different criteria, and others can be very political. My best advice is to not give up, and any volunteer work or fire courses that can be taken can only help in giving you an advantage over the next person."

WHERE CAN I GO FROM HERE?

Promotional opportunities are good in most fire departments, with firefighters typically advancing at regular intervals for the first three to five years as openings occur. Usually the promotion order is: firefighter, driver/engineer, lieutenant, captain, battalion chief, assistant chief, deputy chief, and chief. Firefighters may work three to five years or more before they are promoted to the position of lieutenant.

Advancement generally depends on scores from written examinations, performance on the job, and seniority, although many departments require formal education, such as an associate's degree, for advancement to the rank of lieutenant, captain, and higher. Fire inspectors in fire departments may become officers or heads of fire prevention bureaus. Fire inspection workers in factories may become plant fire marshals or corporate or plant risk managers. After years of service, some firefighters leave the department or retire and become safety consultants.

Having worked as a firefighter for more than 29 years, John says that he has reached his professional goals. "I enjoy being a captain and everything that goes along with working with the guys on my crew and living in the fire station," he explains. "If I were to promote to the next level, I would lose having my own crew and the closeness/camaraderie that goes along with it."

WHAT ARE THE SALARY RANGES?

According to the U.S. Department of Labor, the average annual salary for firefighters was $38,330 in 2004, but salaries vary widely according to region and the type and size of employer. For example, the average mean salary for firefighters in Alaska and Alabama were $29,580 and $30,850, respectively. The same workers in California and New Jersey earned $53,190 and $58,430, respectively. Overall, firefighters earned salaries that ranged from less than $20,200 to $60,760 or more annually.

Salaries also vary according to the size of the city, with firefighters in metropolitan areas typically earning more than their counterparts in rural areas. Another salary factor is the number of firefighters working for the establishment. Generally, the higher the number of workers, the higher the pay.

Most fire departments also provide medical and health care coverage, paid sick leave, and pension and retirement benefits, which include disability or service retirement. Service retirement is generally at half-pay after 20 or 25 years of service. Vacation periods and personal days are provided, and almost all fire

Related Jobs

- alarm investigators
- emergency medical technicians
- fire inspectors and investigators
- fire protection engineers
- fire safety technicians
- lifeguards
- park rangers
- police officers
- ski patrollers

departments furnish appropriate uniforms and safety equipment.

WHAT IS THE JOB OUTLOOK?

Employment of firefighters is expected to increase faster than the average for all occupations through 2014 because of the nation's steadily increasing population and fire protection needs. The number of paid firefighter positions is expected to increase as a percentage of all firefighter jobs, mainly in smaller but growing communities trying to augment their volunteer force with career firefighters. Little growth is expected in large fire departments located in metropolitan areas.

Despite the greater attention to safety in the construction of new buildings, the need for firefighters is not expected to decline. That's because the contents of buildings are still extremely flammable. Buildings used to be built out of paper and wood and cloth, but now construction materials also include polyurethanes and plastics—which create additional challenges for firefighters.

Since most people view firefighters as a necessary service, major cuts in fire department funding are not expected. However, given that many local governments are trimming their budgets, some departments may see small funding cuts. Those cuts are often restored, though, once a major fire or emergency occurs in the community.

"There is always going to be a need for firefighters because most fires and accidents are caused by human error," John says. "In addition, firefighters are usually the first line of defense against any disaster. These days, however, there tend to be more medical calls than fire calls. As cities try to cut costs, firefighters will be forced to perform 'dual' duty and will have to be EMT or paramedic certified."

John strongly recommends a career in firefighting. "The camaraderie with your fellow firefighters is unmatched in any other profession," he explains. "You are able to help others in their time of need and take a chaotic situation and mitigate the dangers. I really enjoy working with and helping others. It's special when a young child comes up to you when you are off duty (at church, at school, or in the community) and recognizes you, and you know that you had a positive influence on that person."

Fire Inspectors and Investigators

SUMMARY

Definition
Fire inspectors help prevent fires by enforcing fire-prevention codes and educating the public about these codes and prevention. Fire investigators study the cause, origin, and circumstances of fires involving loss of life and considerable property damage.

Alternative Job Titles
Arson investigators

Chiefs of fire prevention
Fire marshals
Fire prevention inspectors
Fire prevention officers

Salary Range
$28,000 to $46,000 to $100,000+

Educational Requirements
Some postsecondary training

Certification or Licensing
Recommended

Employment Outlook
About as fast as the average

High School Subjects
Biology
Chemistry
Mathematics

Personal Interests
Figuring out how things work
Helping people: protection
Science

Fire marshals are key members of the fire service. They are responsible for ensuring that people are protected from fires; educating the public about fire safety; and investigating fires when they do happen in order to establish criminal intent and to help prevent future fires. Occasionally, amid all of this responsibility, fire marshals also combine their jobs with some fun. Just such an instance happened when David Lind was selected as one of only 24 fire marshals from across the United States to work at the 2002 Winter Olympic Games in Salt Lake City, Utah. "It was the opportunity of a lifetime," he recalls. "For 10 days,

I worked with 23 of the best fire marshals from across the United States doing what we all did everyday, ensuring that buildings were safe for the public and the employees that enter them. I even had the opportunity to be interviewed by foreign reporters and meet athletes from across the globe."

WHAT DO FIRE INSPECTORS AND INVESTIGATORS DO?

Fire inspectors perform examinations to enforce fire-prevention laws, ordinances, and codes; promote the development and use of effective fire-prevention methods; and provide instruction to the fire department and the general public regarding fire codes and prevention. *Fire investigators* analyze the cause, origin, and circumstances of fires involving loss of life and considerable property damage; interrogate witnesses and prepare investigation reports; and arrest and seek prosecution of arsonists. Fire investigators are also referred to as *arson investigators. Fire inspectors* are also known as *fire prevention inspectors, fire prevention officers*, and *chiefs of fire prevention*. Depending on their responsibilities, fire inspectors and investigators may also collectively be known as *fire marshals.*

Most fire departments are responsible for fire-prevention activities. Fire inspectors inspect buildings and their storage contents for trash and other materials that can ignite easily. They look for worn-out or exposed wiring and for other fire hazards. Inspectors review building and fire-suppression plans to ensure the construction of safe and code-conforming buildings and fire-suppression systems and alarms. They pay close attention to public buildings, such as hospitals, schools, nursing homes, theaters, and hotels, which they inspect regularly. Fire inspectors also ensure that the facility's fire-protection equipment and systems are functioning properly. While inspecting buildings, they might make recommendations on how fire-safety equipment could be used more effectively and provide information regarding the storage of flammable materials, electrical hazards, and other common causes of fires.

Inspectors maintain a variety of reports and records related to fire inspections, code requirements, permits, and training. They also instruct employers, civic groups, schoolchildren, and others on extinguishing small fires, escaping burning buildings, operating fire extinguishers, and establishing evacuation plans.

Fire investigators look for evidence pointing to the causes of fires. Once fires are extinguished, especially if they are of suspicious origin or cause death or injury, investigators look for evidence of arson (fires that are deliberately set for insurance money or other reasons). Investigators first determine whether the fire was incendiary (arson) or accidental, then try to figure out what caused it and how to prevent it. This information is very important to the fire-protection community. In cases of arson, it is the investigator's responsibility to collect information or evidence that can be used to prosecute the fire starter. For example, the investigator must determine what fuel was used to start the fire and in the process may discover devices that were also used. Investigators may submit reports to a district attorney, testify in court, or arrest suspected arsonists (if investigators have police authority). Investigators also gather information from accidental fires to determine where and how the fire started and how it spread. This is important information because it can be used to prevent similar fires in the future.

Fire investigators also interrogate witnesses, obtain statements and other necessary documentation, and preserve and examine physical and circumstantial

Did You Know?

- Fire kills more Americans than all other natural disasters combined.

- Approximately 3,675 civilians died as a result of fire, and another 17,925 were injured as a result of fire in 2005.

- There were 115 firefighters killed while on duty in 2005.

Source: U.S. Fire Administration

evidence. They tour fire scenes and examine debris to collect evidence. Investigators prepare comprehensive reports, provide detailed accounts of investigative procedures, and present findings. They apprehend and arrest arson suspects, as well as seek confinement and control of fire setters and juveniles who set fires. Inspectors also prepare damage estimates for reporting and insurance purposes and compile statistics related to fires and investigations.

WHAT IS IT LIKE TO BE A FIRE INSPECTOR OR INVESTIGATOR?

David Lind is the fire marshal for the North Shore Fire Department, a consolidated department serving seven communities making up most of the northern suburbs of Milwaukee, Wisconsin. He has been a fire marshal for nine years. As fire marshal, David is responsible for both fire

inspection and investigation. David also currently serves as the President of the Wisconsin Fire Inspectors Association. "I chose a career as a fire marshal because it allowed me to use my professional education background and previous work-related skills and training to a greater degree with a higher customer service and safety impact," he explains.

David has many responsibilities during his workday, which usually begins at 8 A.M. "I am responsible for all commercial construction plan review (for new buildings and existing buildings that are being altered or added on to)," he explains, "which could mean anything from looking at construction plans for compliance with the fire code to specific plans dealing with sprinklers, fire alarms, or other life safety systems. Plans are submitted to my office and accepted in my absence. Each day brings the possibility of something new showing up while I'm out of the office during the day or overnight. Specific requests for inspection take priority over plan review."

David also serves as a technical resource for fire code information for the 108 firefighters in his department. "The state of Wisconsin requires all commercial buildings and places of employment to be inspected by the fire department twice a year," he says. "For us, that means approximately 7,200 inspections a year. Out of that 7,200 I will play a role in between 5 and 10 percent. The role I play will depend on the unique circumstances of each inspection. For some it is providing department personnel with specific code sections to apply to a situation they asked about. For others it is going to the structure with the individual or crew to see the situation firsthand and provide on-site information. Lastly, I get involved when the owner of a building has chosen not to respond to the written deficiencies that were identified during the fire inspection. We kind of use a three strikes rule, unless the items compromise the immediate safety of the people inside the building, in which case the fix is ordered to be immediate or within 24 hours. If you are doing plan reviews, the next step in the process as the construction project proceeds is construction inspections." Unless he is out of the office at a meeting or seminar, David is responsible for these inspections. "This can be time consuming depending on the stage of construction and the size of the project," he says.

In addition to inspecting commercial buildings, David is also responsible for fire investigation. "One of the duties every fire department is charged with is determining origin and cause," David says. "A fire can happen any time. It is this particular part of my job that keeps me on call 24 hours a day, seven days a week, 365 days a year," he explains. "The only times I am not on call are those times when I am on vacation or out of town."

David spends approximately 40 to 60 days a year attending meetings, attending or instructing various code-related trainings, and attending at least one nationally sponsored conference a year. "I attend training throughout the year related to building, fire, fire alarm, fire sprinklers, etc.," he explains. "Training is based on two important factors: department bud-

get and necessity. Necessity would best be defined as a new edition of a codebook or standard. The national conference provides me the opportunity to network with people from all over the United States and several other countries. Think of it like a large college campus. There can be people from everywhere discussing hundreds of different topics. It is this conference that has allowed me to see various parts of the United States and Canada."

DO I HAVE WHAT IT TAKES TO BE A FIRE INSPECTOR OR INVESTIGATOR?

Good fire inspectors should enjoy working with people. They should be open to understanding the needs of business owners, but also must strictly enforce

To Be a Successful Fire Inspector Or Investigator, You Should . . .

- enjoy working with people and have good communication skills to explain fire-prevention laws, ordinances, and codes
- have a good eye for detail
- have strong organizational skills
- be in good physical condition
- have integrity

codes if the safety of the public is threatened. They also need to have a good eye for detail and to be able to communicate sometimes complicated fire-prevention laws, ordinances, and codes to the public.

"[Fire] investigators should be well organized in the field as well as in the office," says Robert Duval, a fire investigator for the National Fire Protection Association (NFPA) Fire Investigations Department in Quincy, Massachusetts. "If you are not well organized in the field, you might not get the information you seek, and if your notes and diagrams are a mess, then the report-writing portion of the job will take longer."

Investigators should be in good physical condition to adapt to extreme weather or fire scene conditions and should be able to withstand long hours in unfavorable conditions. Most of all, Robert points out, investigators must have a great deal of integrity. Without this, they will not be credible witnesses in court.

HOW DO I BECOME A FIRE INSPECTOR OR INVESTIGATOR?

Education

High School

Earning a high school diploma is the first step to becoming a fire inspector or investigator. Take classes in physics, biology, and mathematics. Speech and English courses will help you polish your communication skills. David Lind offers the following advice to students: "Learn as much

as you can at whatever you choose to do in life. Remember a couple things: learning does not end when you are no longer in a classroom, and the path you choose now may lead you to things you never imagined. Be open to the possibility."

Postsecondary Training

There are two ways to become a fire inspector. Some fire departments have policies that only those who have served as firefighters can work in the fire-prevention bureau. Other departments want people who are trained primarily for fire prevention. Either way, all students who want to join the fire department, either as an inspector or a firefighter, should take two- or four-year college courses, such as fire service, fire-protection systems, equipment, and fire protection. Specialized fire-prevention classes required for inspectors, such as hazardous materials and processes, flammable liquids, and high-piled stock, can be found through the colleges or the state fire marshal's office. The National Fire Academy (NFA) offers a variety of courses both on and off campus. While the NFA is not an accredited, degree-granting institution, some schools give college credit for NFA courses. Additionally, NFA has partnered with several colleges across the country that offer bachelor's degrees in the areas of fire administration/management and fire-prevention technology. (See the NFA Web site http://www.usfa.dhs.gov/training/nfa/ for more information.)

Fire investigators must have knowledge of fire science, chemistry, engineering, and investigative techniques. However, a fire-related diploma is not always necessary. An engineering certificate with fire-service experience is sufficient in many cases, depending on the job description and whether the position is in the private (corporate) or public (fire department) sector.

"A law enforcement background is helpful. However, not all investigators will have or need the power of arrest," notes Robert Duval. "Many work in the private sector for insurance companies and other interests. In many municipalities and states, the fire marshal's office handles fire investigations, and most investigators are sworn law enforcement officers."

In addition to formal postsecondary training, fire inspectors and investigators must also continue to learn about new developments in the field throughout their careers. Professional membership organizations play a significant role in encouraging their members to stay up to date regarding the field. David Lind, who is president of the Wisconsin Fire Inspectors Association, says that his organization is responsible for providing training for all life safety educators and fire inspectors throughout Wisconsin. "The goal of our association is to provide high-quality education to assist in providing a uniform level of enforcement," he says. "Many states have certification or credential programs to become a fire inspector or fire marshal. Wisconsin is one of those states with a certification class for fire inspector. Many states require a certain amount of class time (continuing education units, or CEUs) or related training over the course of a year or two, or maybe even three years, depending on their

unique requirements. Wisconsin currently does not have such a requirement. Once you pass you certification class, there are currently no additional future requirements for training or education. I believe this will end in the near future. Education only makes you better at what you are out there doing."

David also belongs to national organizations such as the International Fire Marshals Association, the International Arson Investigators Association, and the International Electrical Inspectors Association. "All of these associations have classes designed for the beginner as well as the advanced professional," he says.

Certification and Licensing

Most fire departments look for employees who have been educated in fire science. But you do not have to be certified before being hired. Sometimes, an associate's degree is all that is needed. Most people take the majority of their classes while they are working as fire inspectors.

Local regulations may differ, but generally, fire inspectors obtain certification as a fire prevention officer levels 1 and 2 (sometimes 3) from the office of the state fire marshal. Some states also require fire prevention officer levels 1 and 2. There is a series of classes for each level. The International Code Council also offers examination and certification services for Fire Inspector I and II.

The main certification process for fire investigators is certified fire investigator, which is administered by the International Association of Arson Investigators. There is no straight path to becoming a

What Are Some of the Pros and Cons of Work as a Fire Marshal?

The editors of *What Can I Do Now?: Safety & Security* asked fire marshal David Lind to name his favorite and least favorite aspects of his job.

Pros:

- The job is dynamic and ever changing.
- You leave work every day knowing that you had a direct impact on ensuring a higher level of public safety in buildings, as well as knowing you are providing a safer environment for your fellow firefighters who may have to enter the building in less-than-favorable conditions.
- You have the opportunity to have a positive impact on evacuation planning and strategies used by businesses. Since 9/11, business across the country have taken emergency and evacuation preparedness more seriously.

- You work within the single greatest organization possible, the fire service.
- You are challenged every day to learn more and discover different things as the construction industry and technology changes, and you must integrate those changes with the changing tactics in fire fighting.
- You can work anywhere within the United States, Canada, and even in some foreign countries.

Cons:

- You see the devastation that smoke and fire can do to people, families, and property.
- Your career as a fire marshal in some states is limited to 20 years before you must retire.

fire investigator, and it is not an entry-level job. Most of the investigators who come from fire departments start out in the fire-prevention bureau. Others come from police departments. Fire investigation is a multidisciplinary field, which requires skills in many areas, including firefighting, law enforcement, mechanical engineering, mathematics, and chemical engineering.

Internships and Volunteerships

Although you won't be able to participate in this field until you have received the appropriate training, you can offer your services as a volunteer to your local fire department. Find out if there are any in your area and sign up to volunteer if you meet their requirements. You can also add to your skills by taking CPR and first aid classes.

Labor Unions

Fire inspectors and investigators who have worked as firefighters may be members of the International Association of Firefighters, a labor union of approximately 267,000 members.

WHO WILL HIRE ME?

Fire inspectors are employed by local fire departments and private companies, including factories, sawmills, chemical plants, and universities. Fire investigators are employed by local fire departments, state fire marshal's offices, and private companies. Others work independently as consultants.

Those just starting out in this field will need to determine if they need to gain experience as a professional firefighter before moving into the position of fire inspector. (As mentioned previously, this varies by departments.) To become a fire-fighter, you must pass the local civil service exam, pass physical training, and complete training at the department's training center or academy. Those who have gotten degrees may find information on job openings through their schools' placement centers. Jobs can also be found through organizations, such as the National Fire Protection Association.

WHERE CAN I GO FROM HERE?

Fire inspectors can be promoted to officers or heads of fire-prevention bureaus, fire marshals, or chief building officials. Fire-inspection workers in factories can become plant fire marshals and corporate or plant risk managers. Fire investigators can rise in rank within their department. Many become lieutenants, captains, and fire marshals within their jurisdictions.

Although he is happy in his current position, David Lind plans to seek employment as a state fire marshal in the next five years. "In approximately seven years," he

Related Jobs

- construction inspectors
- detectives
- emergency medical technicians
- firefighters
- fire safety technicians
- forensics experts
- health and regulatory inspectors
- occupational safety and health workers
- park rangers

says, "I hope to retire formally from the fire service. I intend to stay active in my field through several different avenues. I would like to work for the National Fire Protection Association either as a teacher/instructor or as a fire safety code consultant. If I play my cards right I might just do both."

WHAT ARE THE SALARY RANGES?

Inspector salaries depend on two things: if they work in the public or private sector and how large those departments or companies are. Typical salaries range from $30,000 to $45,000 to $75,000 and can increase with experience and years with the organization.

Fire inspectors and investigators earned a median annual salary of $46,340 in 2004, according to the U.S. Department of Labor. Ten percent earned less than $28,420, and the highest 10 percent of all inspectors and investigators earned more than $71,490. As in all occupations, the experts command higher salaries, so private sector investigators' salaries can go much higher (above $100,000) if they are used as national expert witnesses.

WHAT IS THE JOB OUTLOOK?

The outlook for fire inspectors and investigators is about the same as for firefighters. Employment should grow faster than the average for all occupations through 2014, according to the U.S. Department of Labor. "The fire service has been changing and will continue to change over the years," David Lind predicts. "The shift is toward the prevention of fires and the associated injuries, deaths, and property damage as a result of fire. Fire prevention professionals will be in steady demand to [implement] this change in philosophy."

Police Officers

SUMMARY

Definition
Police officers strive to keep people and property safe by enforcing laws, preserving the peace, preventing criminal acts, investigating crimes, arresting violators, and providing assistance.

Alternative Job Titles
Beat officers
Highway patrol officers
Investigative state police officers
Mounted police officers

Patrol officers
State police officers
Traffic police officers

Salary Range
$26,000 to $45,000 to $90,000+

Educational Requirements
High school diploma

Certification or Licensing
None available

Employment Outlook
Faster than the average

High School Subjects
Computer science
Foreign language
Government
Mathematics
Psychology
Sociology

Personal Interests
Exercise/personal fitness
Helping people: emotionally
Helping people: protection
Law
Sports

When we think of police officers, we often think of high-speed chases, drug busts, or the speeding ticket we received from our local police officer. Keeping us safe from crime and maintaining order are huge tasks, but often it's the little unheralded things that police officers do that are the most important. One such example occurred when Master Police Officer Beth Lavin and her partner responded to a domestic violence call.

"The wife had a disabled child, and the husband was threatening her," Beth recalls. "He no longer lived there, but he continued his harassment and threats. The husband also refused to pay child support, we could see that there wasn't a whole lot of food in the house, and it was Thanksgiving."

After Beth and her partner left the house, they decided that they needed to do something for the woman and her child. "We went to the local grocery store," she says, "grabbed a cart (I'm sure people thought it was funny to see two cops pushing a grocery cart!), and filled it with the basic necessities and a full-course Thanksgiving dinner. We paid for this out of our own pockets."

Lingo to Learn

Adam codes Codes used by some during radio communications to describe types of calls. For example, A1 means arrest, A20 means assistance rendered, and A63 means pursuit.

MO: Modus operandi (mode of operation); the standard way, or pattern, in which a particular criminal commits a crime.

probable cause Information developed by an officer to give a reason to arrest, search, or stop and detain a person.

reasonable suspicion The reasons an officer believes a person should be stopped and detained.

surveillance Following, observing, or listening to people for the purpose of obtaining information about criminal activities.

The woman was speechless when Beth and her partner handed her the groceries. "She was crying at how thankful she was," Beth says, "and she invited us to join her for Thanksgiving.

"We didn't have a second thought about helping this woman. I don't think we ever heard from her again, but that's okay. We felt good."

WHAT DOES A POLICE OFFICER DO?

A police officer's duties vary depending on where he or she works. Officers in smaller cities usually perform a wide variety of duties, while officers in larger cities may perform more specialized work, such as identifying firearms, fingerprinting suspects, and investigating criminals. Officers who work for a state government—often known as *state troopers* or *highway patrol officers*—spend much of their time patrolling the highways to enforce the laws and regulations.

Police officers in smaller cities—or patrol officers in larger cities—may spend a considerable amount of time patrolling a beat, usually either on foot or in a police car; however, some police departments have turned to more innovative types of beat patrol transportation, including bicycles, horses, and motorcycles. Through their patrols, officers provide a police presence in their community and remain on the lookout for any unusual or suspicious situations. They may also notice stolen cars, missing children, and wanted suspects or criminals. Officers keep in contact with other officers and their headquarters by using two-way radios. They respond to requests for assistance for a variety of reasons including criminal violations, emergency medical situations, rescues, and traffic control. Officers may issue tickets for such things as traffic and parking violations. They may also arrest drunk drivers and respond to domestic dispute calls.

Police officers in larger cities may perform similar duties, or they may work in more specialized units that respond to certain types of calls or incidents. Typically, police departments in large cities are organized into many divisions, each with squads that do special work. Such units include canine divisions, mounted police, and traffic control. Some officers focus their efforts as members of a rescue team or records unit, while other officers work as plainclothes detectives in criminal investigations. In some cities located near large bodies of water, police officers patrol the marinas and watch wharves, docks, and piers for hazards or criminal activities. Harbor patrols may help people or boats in distress, arrest suspects, or help fight fires near the waterway. Other large departments employ helicopter patrols to assist officers with traffic control and disaster assistance. The helicopters are equipped with special spotlights, so they are effective in apprehending suspects fleeing on foot or by car.

State police officers usually cruise the highways in patrol cars, monitoring the traffic and driving conditions. They issue traffic tickets or warnings to drivers violating traffic laws, provide assistance for drivers with malfunctioning vehicles, and direct traffic through emergencies or construction zones. State police officers also ensure that drivers and vehicles meet state safety regulations. If an accident occurs, officers may administer first aid to victims, request other emergency personnel, and direct traffic around the site. *Investigative state police officers* work to determine the causes of accidents. In addition, some state police departments serve as the primary law enforcement agency for communities that do not have a city or county police force.

Regardless of where they work, most police officers are highly trained in a variety of areas, such as firearms use, vehicle pursuit, and self-defense. Officers must carry a gun with them on duty, and many

officers wear bullet- and knife-resistant vests. All police officers are required to document their work by writing reports—which can involve many hours of paperwork—about their responses to various types of calls. In addition, officers are sometimes called to testify in court about their knowledge of cases in which they have been involved.

Police officers may experience stressful and dangerous situations. Officers are responsible for subduing and arresting violent people, including armed robbers and murderers. They try to restore peace and order during riots. They also attempt to rescue or aid victims of automobile accidents, fires, drownings, and more. Many police officers are exposed to death, whether by accident, suicide, or homicide. Officers also must adhere to local, state, and federal procedures for making arrests, searching and seizing property, and upholding citizens' civil rights.

The demanding duties, working conditions, and hours of a police officer can be very stressful for the officer, as well as for his or her family. Besides the stress and danger, the physical working conditions may not be pleasant. Police officers respond to calls in all weather conditions, which means they are exposed to blizzards, hurricanes, heat, and other extreme conditions. The work can also be very difficult and tiring, requiring officers to stay in top physical shape. They may be required to engage in a high-speed chase by car, or a strenuous chase on foot. Police officers also must be prepared to defend themselves, or even shoot a person in some cases. Between their bullet-resistant vest and duty belt—which holds tools such as a radio, handcuffs, pepper spray, and a weapon—police officers easily carry 20 pounds of extra weight.

WHAT IS IT LIKE TO BE A POLICE OFFICER?

Beth Lavin has been a sheriff's deputy in King County, Washington, for 14 years. "I know this may sound like a cliché," she says, "but I really enjoy being out there with the community, trying to make some kind of a difference. I know I can't change the world, but maybe just my little part of it in some way."

Beth is a master police officer working patrol on day shift in the contract city of Shoreline. "A contract city," she explains, "is when a city incorporates, but cannot afford its own police department; they hire the sheriff's office to work there." Beth's shift begins at 6:00 A.M. and ends at 2:00 P.M. When I get into work," she says, "I check our information bulletins on who has outstanding warrants, who is wanted, and other people to look out for. Then, I get on my laptop and also read other officer reports from the previous night to look for certain crime patterns or subjects to look for." She also catches up on paperwork during this time and participates in a "roll call" where her shift sergeant covers important issues of the day. Then Beth goes on patrol. "We answer 911 calls and try to be proactive in the community. Community policing is such a big thing for us. It's important to know the community and the business owners and to keep a great relationship going."

In addition to her regular duties, Beth also serves on the Oral Board Panel for the King County Sheriff's Office, "which," she says, "entails interviewing prospective lateral or entry-level candidates who want to become deputies with our department." She usually spends about two to three days doing this task. "I am also a member of the extradition team, which picks up prisoners from throughout the United States to bring them back to Washington for trial, and a field training officer. I train new recruits who have just come out of the academy and are now on the street."

Beth says that one of things she likes best about her job is that it is different every day. "Everyday you'll get calls that are different from the day before. Maybe it's the same type of call, but it might be

---

To Be a Successful Police Officer, You Should . . .

- be honest and trustworthy
- have good communication skills
- be patient, fair, and a good listener
- have good physical health, stamina, and agility
- be able to think quickly on your feet and make solid decisions
- enjoy meeting and working with people

handled in a different way. You could be just driving around one minute, and then the next you're chasing down a bad guy!"

DO I HAVE WHAT IT TAKES TO BE A POLICE OFFICER?

Most police officers agree that it takes a special kind of person to both enjoy the profession and be successful. High on the list of desirable personal qualifications is honesty, which officers need in order to be trusted with peoples' lives, families, money, and property. "Integrity is huge," says Kitty McDonald, a detective in the Burbank Police Department and a police officer for 20 years. (She is also the wife of Dan McDonald, who is profiled later in this chapter.) "Can I as a partner trust you? Can the citizens trust you? Are the reports that I write about an incident (which could send someone to jail) factual?" Good communication is another key quality, because police officers spend much of their time talking to people of various ethnic backgrounds, cultures, religions, and beliefs.

Learning to be a good, fair listener is important because police officers often act as mediators and try to resolve conflicts between people. Police officers also must be able to think quickly and make solid decisions, sometimes on the spur of the moment. Patience and diplomacy are also good characteristics for officers to develop.

And since officers deal with the public on a daily basis, they should enjoy meeting and working with people.

You may be attracted to the Hollywood version of law enforcement—constant car chases, shootouts, and drama. But there are many routine, unglamorous aspects to the job, so if you're interested in law enforcement solely because of the authority and glory it brings, you may be in for a rude awakening. The actions of police officers are often carefully scrutinized and criticized. If you're in the profession for the wrong reason, the drawbacks to the job will probably overshadow the positive aspects.

Police officers must pass written, physical, and oral tests to measure their intelligence, judgment, and knowledge. They may also be required to pass a vision test, background check, and drug use test. Police officers must be citizens of the United States, they must meet minimum age requirements (usually 20 or 21), and in some cases they must live in the community in which they are seeking employment. Officers also need a driver's license and excellent driving record.

Women make up only 24 percent of police officers and security guards in the United States, according to the U.S. Department of Labor. This gender inequity may present special challenges to women police officers. "There are only 11 females in my entire department," says Kitty McDonald. "And when I started with the department . . . there were only eight women—so you can see that we haven't really grown much in number over the years." Despite stereotypes, women have consistently proven themselves as police officers, and the attitudes of the public and male police officers have improved in the last decade or two. Kitty offers the following advice to females who are interested in becoming police officers: "Get in shape, stay in shape, and don't expect that the department you work for will change its standards to accommodate you. You also need to understand that there are still people—both citizens and a few officers—out there who don't think a female should be an officer. In this instance, you just have to deal with it and say, 'you know, that's your problem,' and do your job to the best of your abilities."

HOW DO I BECOME A POLICE OFFICER?

Education

Beth Lavin wanted to become a police officer from the time she was a little girl, but knew while in her teens that she was not yet old enough to apply to the force. Instead, she joined the army when she was 17. "That was a great growing-up time for me," she recalls, "meeting and interacting with people from all different backgrounds. I received a lot of life experience through the military, and I have no regrets. I was very motivated to be the best in the army. I was in the Honor Guard and was named soldier and NCO [non-commissioned officer] of the month. I obtained the rank of staff sergeant in just 10 years, which I thought was very successful. No, I wasn't an MP [military police] in the army, I didn't think waving people through a gate was challenging, so I first came in as a light wheel mechanic,

then I ended my career as a supply sergeant in a BlackHawk Unit with a $15 million budget. The army could be very stressful at times, but I learned so much about dealing with stress and getting through it."

High School

Since almost all police departments require applicants to be a high school graduate, plan on it as a necessary requirement. To prepare for a job as a police officer, it may help to take classes in psychology, sociology, English, law, U.S. government, history, chemistry, physics, foreign languages, and driver education. Computer instruction is becoming more and more important as police departments across the country are using computer technology in a growing number of ways. Mathematics is also sometimes overlooked as an important subject for future police officers. "Math is very important," Kitty McDonald says, "especially if you work in an area such as the traffic division, where you will be diagramming accidents. These officers use algebra, trigonometry, and related courses to create factual diagrams of accidents. They have to base their drawings on what they see from a photograph because few people or no one witnessed the accident. And when these specialists retire from the police department, they are hired by insurance agencies and can get paid very well, or they can work for a law firm that does accident reconstructions." Taking physical education classes and participating in sports is also key. "Police officers need to stay in good physical shape

(continued on page 108)

An Interesting Career Opportunity

Dan McDonald has been a deputy sheriff for the Los Angeles County Sheriff's Department for nearly 22 years. (He is also the husband of Kitty McDonald, who is profiled earlier in this chapter.) Early in his career, he worked as a custody officer in the county's jails and, until recently, worked as a patrol officer. He recently took on a new challenge—working in the Civil Litigation Unit of his department. He was kind enough to discuss his new career with the editors of *What Can I Do Now?: Safety & Security*.

Q. What are your duties in the Civil Litigation Unit?

A. I work with our county counsel and contracted lawyers to defend Los Angeles County in lawsuits. When a lawsuit is brought against the county there will be discovery motions where the plaintiff's lawyer will say "I want to see any records or reports that are pertinent to what happened." It is my job to find these documents so that our lawyers can provide them for discovery. In my unit, eight of us specialize in incidents that occur in the county's jails, and three deputies specialize in traffic-related cases. Although I'm new to the field and still learning, I really love the job.

Q. Take us through a typical day on the job.

A. When I get to work, I look at my phone, which is lit up like a Christmas tree. I gather all of my messages about requests from lawyers and law firms. I check e-mails for requests for discovery-related documents. I also have a stack of mail waiting for me

from lawyers—discovery motions, verification letters that need to be signed, and so on. And once I have my requests, I just go out and work each case. I am currently handling approximately 75 active lawsuits. I am responsible for handling any lawsuit that comes in regarding four jails: three jails in downtown Los Angeles (the Men's Central Jail, the Twin Towers Correctional Facility, and the Inmate Reception Center) and one in southern Los Angeles (Century Regional Detention Facility).

This job is completely different from any other job I've had in law enforcement. It's a job that when you leave at the end of the day, your work is not done. When you come back the next morning, you have the remainder of the previous day's work to do, plus new lawsuits to begin working on. It just never stops.

Q. What type of materials do the lawyers typically request?

A. On average, lawyers request any and all police reports regarding the incident. For example, let's say the lawsuit is about the use of force against an inmate that involved three or four county employees (use-of-force reports are very common, and lawsuits behind them are almost automatic). Lawyers typically ask for injury reports that were written about the inmates. They might also request each deputy's personnel records to find out if anybody has a history of using force that seems to fall outside the department's parameters on acceptable use

(continued on next page)

(continued from previous page)

of force. They request logs as to who was on duty at the time of the incident or logs detailing the activities that occurred in a certain section of the jail during the time of the incident. Other items that might be requested include audiotapes, videotapes, photographs of the scene or an individual's injuries, homicide packets (if an inmate dies in the county's custody), and booking jackets. I may also be asked to set up depositions with the deputies and custody assistants who were involved in the incident.

Q. Has your past experience in law enforcement helped you succeed in this job?

A. Absolutely. My background definitely has helped me to understand what I'm looking for—who to contact, where to look for documents, and so on. But this is not a job for someone with only a few years of experience in the department, unless he or she has a specialized legal background.

Q. Where would you like to be professionally in 5 or 10 years?

A. In 5 or 10 years, I'd like to be retired. One great thing about working in this field is that if you start your career early enough, and work 25 or 30 years, you're only about 55 when you retire. That's a nice early age to retire. That's one of the great things about working in law enforcement.

because our jobs are very physically demanding," Kitty says. "It doesn't seem like that because sometimes we sit all day, but there will be that one time where you have to take off running and get in a fight. If you get in good condition while you're in high school, you'll maintain it the rest of your life."

You've heard it before: "This will go on your permanent record!" Law enforcement is one of the few careers where this statement is actually true. "Kids think that what they do while in high school—good or bad—doesn't matter," Kitty says, "but high school is really a base that we look at, especially for aspiring police in their early 20s. Kids need to stay clear of drugs, excel in aca-

demics, watch their driving record, maintain a good record at work (if they have a job), and make ethical choices. We all know that people make mistakes, but young people need to remember that, within the next three or four years of their lives, someone is going to be looking at their background, seeing what they did or didn't do, and asking 'How mature was this person then? Did he or she make good or bad choices? Will he or she make the same choices when hired in the department?'"

One thing high school students can do to prepare themselves for a career in law enforcement is to get involved with their community and try to improve it. Volunteer your talents to a local police department, government agency, or in a retirement home or hospital.

Postsecondary Training

While most police departments don't yet require a college degree, the trend is heading in that direction. Several states—including New York, New Jersey, North Dakota, and Iowa—and numerous municipalities require applicants to have a two- or four-year college degree. More and more junior colleges, colleges, and universities are offering programs in law enforcement or administration of justice. While fewer than 5 percent of police officers in 1970 had a college degree, more than a quarter of all police officers today hold a college degree. "Our department is very big on officers having their degree—especially as it relates to improving a deputy's eligibility for promotion," says Dan McDonald. "Some people may be surprised to learn that the degrees often sought by my department are not in criminal justice, but in areas such as business administration, accounting, and the humanities. Departments are looking for business-minded individuals to run things." While Dan strongly encourages high school students to go to college, he doesn't necessarily believe that a college degree should be a prerequisite for being hired by a department. "I don't know if a law enforcement officer has to have a degree," he says. "I don't think it's a bad thing, but some people may tell you 'just because you have a college degree doesn't mean that you will be a good cop.'"

After they are hired, most officers in state and large local police departments go through training at a police academy, usually for eight to 14 weeks. Such training programs are intense and include classroom instruction on topics such as constitutional law and civil rights, state laws and local ordinances, and accident investigation. Dan describes his training at the Los Angeles County Sheriff's Academy as intense. "I graduated two weeks after the '84 Los Angeles Olympics ended," he recalls, "and I can tell you, I didn't see two minutes of it!" Recruits may also receive training and supervised experience in patrol, traffic control, weapons and firearms use, self-defense, first aid, safe driving procedures, physical fitness, and emergency response. After the training, new officers usually serve a probationary period lasting from three to six months. In smaller towns, new hires may be trained on the job—rather than at an academy—by working with an experienced officer.

Internships and Volunteerships

Students who attend postsecondary training programs will be required to participate in an internship with a police or other law enforcement department. Internships, which typically last from four months to a year, will provide you an excellent introduction to the everyday world of police work.

Most police departments have a community outreach program or recruitment program and will visit with interested individuals. Many departments also have a "ride along" program, through which people can ride in a patrol car with a police officer and observe his or her working conditions and duties. High school graduates may learn more about the life of a police officer by becoming a police cadet in a large city police department. Cadets are paid employees who work part time performing clerical or other duties for a police department. They may be allowed to attend training courses, and then apply to become a regular police officer once they are old enough. In addition, some police departments hire college students as interns.

Labor Unions

Many police officers who work for cities belong to the city's bargaining unit, which negotiates city employees' salaries and benefits. In addition, some police officers belong to the National Fraternal Order of Police or the International Union of Police Associations (AFL-CIO).

In addition to unions, many police officers are members of professional associations, which represent the professional interests of their members. Major police associations include the National Sheriffs' Association (NSA), the International Association of Chiefs of Police (IACP), the Law Enforcement Association of Asian Pacifics (LEAAP), the National Black Police Association (NBPA), and the International Association of Women Police (IAWP). Beth Lavin is a member of the IAWP. "Last year," she says, "I was selected to be the

Region 9 Coordinator with the association, which includes Washington, Oregon, Idaho, Alaska, Montana, and Wyoming. I will be the director for the 47th annual IAWP training conference in Seattle in 2009."

WHO WILL HIRE ME?

The United States has more than 18,000 municipal police agencies, 3,000 county sheriff departments, and 1,200 state and federal police agencies. There were approximately 842,000 police and detectives employed in the United States in 2004. Eighty percent were employed at the local level, 12 percent at the state level, and 6 percent at the federal level. Others work for educational services, rail transportation, and contract investigation and security services.

Local civil service rules and state laws govern the hiring of police officers in almost all large cities and most small cities. Contact the department directly to find out where to apply for a position. Some cities offer a local civil service office or examining board. In small cities, candidates usually apply directly to the department. If you are interested in working for a state or federal government, contact the agency to inquire about the application process.

Check law enforcement trade journals for advertisements. The Internet offers many law enforcement employment sites and the Web sites of specific law enforcement agencies. Local newspapers also advertise police officer positions.

Advancement Possibilities

- *Sergeants* are first-line supervisors who work directly with the police officers. They evaluate and train officers, make assignments, and schedule shifts.

- *Lieutenants* are mid-level managers who occasionally work the streets. They concentrate more on personnel issues and the management of patrol teams.

- *Captains* oversee a major unit within a department, develop a budget, and approve expenditures. In some departments this is an appointed position.

Police officers may also find employment working at a college or university. Others work for private companies providing security or investigative services.

WHERE CAN I GO FROM HERE?

In general, advancement is determined by length of service, job performance, formal education and training courses, and test scores. Depending on the department, promotions usually become available six months to three years after hiring. The progression of promotion is typically police officer, detective, sergeant, lieutenant, captain, assistant chief, and chief, depending on the department's structure.

Larger departments usually have additional top-level management positions, such as division, bureau, or department directors. These positions, and that of chief, are often made by direct political appointment.

"I'll probably work as a police officer until I'm 50 years old," predicts Beth Lavin, "which is nine years from now. I'd like to get back into a specialty unit like our domestic identification unit at my precinct for a couple of years. My favorite thing is to be on patrol though. I love being on the street."

In five years or so, Kitty McDonald hopes to be promoted to the position of sergeant. "That's what my lieutenant and sergeant are pushing our detail for," she says. "I can see myself as a sergeant working patrol. I don't know if I'd go much farther than that. Supposedly, everyone, including the chief, would tell you that sergeant is the best position in the department. After I retire, I may want to get into teaching. I was a paramedic prior to becoming a police officer, so nursing is something I've also thought about."

WHAT ARE THE SALARY RANGES?

According to the U.S. Department of Labor, police officers earned an annual average salary of $45,210 in 2004; the lowest 10 percent earned less than $26,900 a year, while the highest 10 percent earned $68,880 or more annually. Police officers in supervisory positions earned median salaries of $61,010 a year in 2002, with a low of less than $36,340 and a high of more than $90,070. Salaries for police officers range widely based on geographic location. Police departments in the West and North generally pay more than those in the South.

Police officers' benefits include vacation and sick leave, medical insurance, compensatory time/holiday pay, retirement, deferred compensation, tuition reimbursement, and overtime, which is common and can be significant.

WHAT IS THE JOB OUTLOOK?

Employment of police officers and detectives will grow about as fast as the average through 2014, according to the U.S. Department of Labor. "It's a very good time to become a police officer," Beth Lavin says. "For example, my department has 40 openings right now. That's huge! We hire every month, and plan to for the next few years. It's the turnaround thing: officers retiring, medical retirements, etc. I know that other departments in the United States are in a hiring frenzy as well." Kitty McDonald agrees. "There will always be police work because there will always be bad people in the world," she says. "The job has many rewards: most people appreciate and respect what you do, the pay and benefits are good, and you are guaranteed a job for your career unless you really mess up."

Related Jobs

- air marshals
- border patrol officers
- corrections officers
- customs officials
- deputy sheriffs
- detectives
- drug enforcement agency agents
- FBI special agents
- fire inspectors
- fire investigators
- fish and game wardens
- immigration officers
- military police officers
- private investigators
- Secret Service special agents
- security officers
- sheriffs
- special agents
- state highway patrol officers
- U.S. marshals
- wildlife agents

The salaries and benefits of police officers are viewed as attractive by many and the number of qualified candidates is expected to continue to exceed the number of available positions. As a result, the field is becoming more and more competitive, with applicants bringing more substantial resumes to the screening process. Candidates with college training will likely prove to be more competitive than those with high school diplomas, although relevant experience also can help.

Opportunities for police officers are expected to be better in urban commu-nities where crime is somewhat higher and officers' pay is relatively low. Depart-ments in these areas are having trouble recruiting high-quality police officer candidates.

Secret Service Special Agents

SUMMARY

Definition
U.S. Secret Service special agents work to protect the president and other political leaders of the United States, as well as heads of foreign states or governments when they are visiting the United States. Special agents also investigate financial crimes and computer-based attacks on our nation's infrastructure.

Alternative Job Titles
None

Salary Range
$24,677 to $54,221 to $158,100

Educational Requirements
Bachelor's degree

Certification or Licensing
None available

Employment Outlook
About as fast as the average

High School Subjects
Computer science
English (writing/literature)
Foreign language
Government
Physical education
Psychology

Personal Interests
Computers
Current events
Exercise/personal fitness
Helping people: protection
Law
Travel

Bands play and crowds cheer as the president of the United States strides from Air Force One to a waiting armored limousine at the Pittsburgh Airport. Once he is safely in the car, the motorcade begins driving to the site of a convention where the president will speak.

Secret Service special agent Norm Jarvis is riding in the car behind the president's limo. It's quiet inside the car, except for the occasional crackle of the radio, alerting the agents to potential problems. Jarvis and the other agents look intently out the windows at the streets lined with people hoping to catch a glimpse of the president.

"There's a group of protesters ahead on the left," he tells his coworkers. On the right side of the road he sees a group of waving school children holding a banner that reads, "Stop here, Mr. President!"

Things are quiet for the next few minutes. Then suddenly Jarvis hears a loud "Bang! Bang!" His heart jumps for a second before he realizes the sound is not gunfire but merely a backfire from one of the police motorcycles driving alongside the car. He breathes deeply for a moment, then focuses his mind back on the job at hand—protecting the president of the United States.

WHAT DOES A SPECIAL AGENT DO?

Secret Service special agents are charged with two missions: protecting U.S. leaders or visiting foreign heads of state, and investigating, according to its Web site, "violations of laws relating to counterfeiting of obligations and securities of the United States; financial crimes that include, but are not limited to, access device fraud, financial institution fraud, identity theft, computer fraud; and computer-based attacks on our nation's financial, banking, and telecommunications infrastructure." Special agents are empowered to carry and use firearms, execute warrants, and make arrests.

Besides the president, vice president, and their immediate families, special agents work to ensure the safety of a number of other individuals (see sidebar, "The Secret Service: Protective Services, Yesterday and Today"). Special agents work continually to protect certain U.S. leaders, like the president, and when a government summit is held in the United States or abroad, special agents are responsible for protecting either the visiting foreign leaders, or the American leaders who have traveled to a foreign country.

When assigned to a permanent protection duty—for the president, for example—special agents are usually assigned to the Washington, D.C., area. They are responsible for planning and executing protective operations for their protectee at all times. Agents can also be assigned to a temporary protective duty to provide protection for candidates or visiting for-

eign dignitaries. In either case, an advance team of special agents surveys each site that will be visited by the protectee. Based on their survey, the team determines how much manpower and what types of equipment are needed to provide protection. The team members identify hospitals and evacuation routes, and they work closely with local police, fire, and rescue units to develop the protection plan and to determine emergency routes and procedures, should the need arise. Then a command post is set up with secure communications to act as the communication center for protective activities. The post monitors emergencies and keeps participants in contact with each other.

Before the protectees arrive, the lead advance agent coordinates all law enforcement representatives participating in the visit. The assistance of military, federal, state, county, and local law enforcement organizations is a vital part of the entire security operation. Personnel are told where they will be posted and are alerted to specific problems associated with the visit. Intelligence information is discussed and emergency measures are outlined. Just prior to the arrival of the protectee, checkpoints are established and access to the secure area is limited. After the visit, special agents analyze every step of the protective operation, record unusual incidents, and suggest improvements for future operations.

When assigned to an investigative duty, special agents investigate threats against Secret Service protectees. They also work to detect and arrest people committing any offense relating to coins, currency, stamps, government bonds, checks, credit card fraud, computer fraud, false identification crimes, and other obligations or securities of the United States. Special agents also investigate violations of the Federal Deposit Insurance Act, the Federal Land Bank Act, and the Government Losses in Shipment Act. Special agents assigned to an investigative duty usually work in one of the Secret Service's 125 domestic and foreign field offices. Agents assigned to investigative duties in a field office are often called out to serve on a temporary protective operation.

Special agents assigned to investigate financial crimes may also be assigned to one of the Secret Service's three divisions in Washington, D.C., or they may receive help from the divisions while conducting an investigation from a field office. The Counterfeit Division constantly reviews the latest reprographic and lithographic technologies to remain a step ahead of counterfeiters. The Criminal Investigative Division aids special agents in their investigation of electronic crimes involving credit cards, computers, cell and regular telephones, narcotics, illegal firearms trafficking, homicide, and other crimes. The Forensic Services Division coordinates forensic science activities within the Secret Service. The division analyzes evidence such as documents, fingerprints, photographs, and video and audio recordings.

The Secret Service employs a number of specialists such as electronics engineers, communications technicians, research psychologists, computer experts, armorers, intelligence analysts, polygraph examiners, forensic experts, and security specialists.

Lingo to Learn

choke point A potential ambush site—like a bridge—where a protectee or motorcade may be more vulnerable to attack.

protective bubble A 360-degree virtual boundary of safety that the Secret Service maintains around each of its protectees. Special agents work to ensure that nothing dangerous penetrates the bubble.

protectee A person—usually a political leader of the United States or a foreign dignitary—that the Secret Service is responsible for protecting. Protectees may also include the spouse or family of the primary protectee.

WHAT IS IT LIKE TO BE A SECRET SERVICE SPECIAL AGENT?

For more than 20 years, Norm Jarvis has been a special agent for the Secret Service. He has protected a variety of U.S. political leaders including past presidents Clinton, Carter, Ford, and Nixon. He has also protected foreign dignitaries including the president of Sudan and the prime minister of Israel. In addition, Norm has investigated criminal activity in a number of cities.

While his primary responsibility is to investigate crimes, Norm is called out regularly to protect a political or foreign leader. During those times, he serves as a member of a team of special agents who work to ensure that there is always a "protective bubble" surrounding the protectee, regardless of whether he or she is in a moving or stationary location. Protective operations can be complicated, with special agents working together around the clock, using intelligence and special technologies, and working in conjunction with local authorities to make sure the protectee is safe. "We don't believe anybody can do bodyguard work just by walking around with somebody," Norm says. "Scowls and large muscles don't mean a lot if somebody is bound and determined to kill you." While special agents don't change their protective techniques when they work overseas, they often work in conjunction with foreign security agencies. "Other security forces usually defer to the Secret Service, which is considered a premier security agency," Norm says.

When Norm is not on a protective assignment, he spends his time investigating a variety of crimes. Special agents assigned to smaller field offices typically handle a wide variety of criminal investigations. But special agents usually work for a specialized squad in a field office, handling specific investigations like counterfeit currency, forgery, and financial crimes. Special agents may receive case referrals from the Secret Service headquarters, from other law enforcement agencies, or through their own investigations. Investigating counterfeit money requires extensive undercover operations and surveillance. Special agents usually work with the U.S. Attorney's Office and

To Be a Successful Secret Service Special Agent, You Should . . .

- have strong ethics, morals, and virtues
- be confident and honest, with no criminal background
- be flexible and willing to work away from home at a moment's notice
- be highly intelligent and able to act quickly in an emergency
- be willing to risk injury or loss of life in the course of your protective duties

local law enforcement for counterfeit cases. Through their work, special agents detect and seize millions of dollars of counterfeit money each year—some of which is produced overseas. Special agents working in a fraud squad often receive complaints or referrals from banking or financial institutions that have been defrauded. Fraud investigations involve painstaking and long-term investigations to reveal the criminals, who are usually organized groups or individuals hiding behind false identifications. Special agents working for forgery squads are often referred to cases from banks or local police departments that have discovered incidents of forgery.

Protective and investigative assignments can keep a special agent away from home for long periods of time, depending on the situation. Preparations for the president's visits to cities in the United States generally take no more than a week. But a large event attracting foreign dignitaries—the Asian Pacific Conference in the state of Washington, for example—can take months to plan. Special agents at field offices assigned to investigate crimes are called out regularly to serve temporary protective missions. During campaign years, agents typically serve three-week protective assignments, work three weeks back at their field office, and then start the process over again. Special agents always work at least 40 hours a week and often work a minimum of 50 hours each week.

DO I HAVE WHAT IT TAKES TO BE A SPECIAL AGENT?

The Secret Service is looking for smart, upstanding citizens who will favorably represent the U.S. government. The agency looks for people with strong ethics, morals, and virtues—and then they teach them how to be a special agent. "You can be a crackerjack lawyer, but have some ethical problems in your background, and we wouldn't hire you as an agent even though we would love to have your expertise," Norm says.

Special agents also need dedication, which can be demonstrated through a candidate's grade point average in high school and college. And applicants must have a drug-free background. Even experimental drug use can be a reason to dis-

miss an applicant from the hiring process. Special agents also need to be confident and honest—with no criminal background. "It's important as a representative of the President's Office that you conduct yourself well, that you look good, and that you're able to command some respect," Norm says. "Anything even as minor as shoplifting is an indicator of a personality problem."

Since special agents must travel for their jobs—Norm spends about 30 percent of his time on the road—interested applicants should be flexible and willing to be away from home. Norm says the traveling is one of the downfalls of the job, often requiring him to leave his wife and two children with a moment's notice.

One of the drawbacks of being a special agent is the potential danger involved. A special agent was shot in the stomach in 1981 during an assassination attempt on President Ronald Reagan. Other agents have been killed on the job in helicopter accidents, surveillance assignments, and protective operations, to name a few.

But the benefits outweigh the drawbacks for most agents. For Norm, the excitement and profound importance of his work gives him great job satisfaction. "There are times when you are involved in world history and you witness history being made, or you are present when historical decisions are being made, and you feel privileged to be a part of making history, albeit behind the scenes and never recognized for it," he says, noting how fascinating he finds the job. However, the job is not always glamorous,

<table>
<tr><td>

The Secret Service: Protective Services, Yesterday and Today

The Secret Service was established in 1865 to suppress the counterfeiting of U.S. currency. After the assassination of President William McKinley in 1901, the Secret Service was directed by Congress to protect the president of the United States.

Today, it is the Secret Service's responsibility to protect:

- The president, vice president, and their immediate families.

- Former presidents and their spouses for 10 years after they leave office. (Spousal protection terminates in the case of remarriage, but individuals elected prior to January 1, 1997, receive lifetime protection.)

- Children of former presidents until they are 16 years old.

- Visiting heads of foreign states or governments and their spouses traveling with them.

- Official representatives of the United States who are performing special missions abroad.

- Major presidential and vice presidential candidates, and, within 120 days of the general presidential election, their spouses.

</td></tr>
</table>

HOW DO I BECOME A SPECIAL AGENT?

Education

High School

You can help prepare for a career as a special agent by doing well in high school. You may receive special consideration by the Secret Service if you have computer training, which is needed to investigate computer fraud, or if you can speak a foreign language, which is useful during investigations and while protecting visiting heads of state or U.S. officials who are working abroad. Specialized skills are highly regarded in electronics, forensics, and other investigative areas. Aside from school, doing something unique and positive for your city or neighborhood, or becoming involved in community organizations can improve your chances of being selected by the Secret Service.

The Secret Service also offers the Stay-In-School Program for high school students. The program allows students who meet financial eligibility guidelines to earn money and some benefits by working part-time, usually in a clerical job for the agency. There are many requirements and application guidelines for this program, so contact the Secret Service's Stay-In-School office at 202-406-5800 or go online at http://www.secretservice.gov/opportunities_stay-in-school.shtml.

Postsecondary Training

The Secret Service recruits special agents at the GS-5, GS-7, and GS-9 grade levels. You can qualify at the GS-5 level in one of

and can be "like going out in your backyard in your best suit and standing for three hours," according to one of Norm's coworkers.

three ways: obtain a four-year degree from an accredited college or university; work for at least three years in a criminal investigative or law enforcement field, and gain knowledge and experience in applying laws relating to criminal violations; or obtain an equivalent combination of education and experience. You can qualify at the GS-7 or GS-9 level by achieving superior academic scores (defined as a grade point average of at least 2.95 on a 4.0 scale), going to graduate school and studying a directly related field, or gaining an additional year of criminal investigative experience.

All newly hired special agents go through 12 weeks of training at the Federal Law Enforcement Training Center in Glynco, Georgia, or Artesia, New Mexico, and then 16 weeks of specialized training at the James J. Rowley Training Center in Laurel, Maryland. During training, new agents take comprehensive courses in protective techniques, criminal and constitutional law, criminal investigative procedures, use of scientific investigative devices, first aid, the use of firearms, and defensive measures. Special agents also learn about collecting evidence, surveillance techniques, undercover operations, and courtroom demeanor. Specialized training includes skills such as firefighting and protection aboard airplanes. The classroom study is supplemented by on-the-job training, and special agents go through advanced in-service training throughout their careers.

New special agents usually begin work at the field office where they first applied. Their initial work is investigative in nature and is closely supervised. After about five years, agents are usually transferred to a protection assignment.

Internships and Volunteerships

The Secret Service offers the Cooperative Education Program as a way for the agency to identify and train highly motivated students for a career as a special agent. Participants of the paid program learn more about the Secret Service and gain on-the-job training, with the possibility of working full time for the Secret Service upon graduation. The two-year work-study program includes classroom and hands-on training that prepares students for the following Secret Service careers: accountant, budget analyst, computer research specialist, computer specialist, electronics engineer, intelligence research specialist, management specialist, personnel management specialist, telecommunications specialist, and visual information specialist. Students working towards a bachelor's degree must complete 1,040 hours of study-related work requirements.

To be considered for the program, you must: be enrolled full time in an accredited educational program; be enrolled in your school's cooperative education program; maintain a 3.0 grade point average in either undergraduate or graduate studies; be a U.S. citizen; be enrolled in a field of study related to the position for which you are applying; pass a drug test; and pass a preliminary background investigation and possibly a polygraph test.

Students in the program work part time, which is between 16 and 32 hours a

Advancement Possibilities

Assistants to the special agent in charge supervise a squad of agents in a field office.

Special agents in charge oversee a field office or protective detail.

Deputy assistant directors help manage the Secret Service's headquarters, field offices, and protective details.

week. They may work full time during holidays and school breaks. They receive some federal benefits including a pension plan, low-cost life and health insurance, annual vacation and sick leave, holiday pay, awards, and promotions.

You must submit a variety of forms to apply for this program, so contact the Secret Service's Cooperative Education Program coordinator at 202-435-5800 for more information or go online at http://www.secretservice.gov/opportunities_co-op.shtml. You may also be able to apply through the cooperative education program at your school.

WHO WILL HIRE ME?

Norm didn't set out to become a special agent. As a teenager, he admired a neighbor who worked as a deputy sheriff. As Norm grew older and had to make decisions about college and work, he realized that he wanted to go into law enforcement. At the age of 18, he volunteered to go into the U.S. Army to train with the military police. When Norm left the service, he used his VA benefits to help him get a bachelor's degree in psychology from Westminster College. "I have an innate interest in why people do the things they do," he says. Norm also earned a master's degree in public administration, and he spent eight years working as a police officer before he decided to apply with the Secret Service. He wasn't satisfied with his police officer's salary and was tired of what he describes as the "day-to-day emotional trauma of being an officer." Norm loved to travel and was impressed by some special agents he had met, so he decided that becoming a special agent would be a way for him to advance professionally and work in an exciting position. He applied for the job and began working as a special agent assigned to Salt Lake City in 1984.

The Secret Service warns that because they have many well-qualified applicants and few anticipated vacancies, the likelihood that you will get hired is limited. On top of that, the hiring process can take up to a year—or longer—because of the thoroughness of the selection process. All special agent candidates must pass a thorough personal interview, the Treasury Enforcement Agent Examination or the U.S. Marshal's Enforcement Examination, a physical examination, a polygraph test, drug screening, and an extensive background investigation. The most qualified candidates then undergo in-depth interviews.

The successful applicant must be in excellent physical condition, with weight proportionate to his or her height. Candidates' distant vision must be at least 20/60 in each eye uncorrected, and 20/20 in each eye corrected; near vision must be at least 20/40 corrected. Newly appointed special agents must be at least 21 years old and less than 37 old when they are appointed, and they must be U.S. citizens. They may be assigned to work anywhere in the United States, and throughout their careers agents will travel frequently and be reassigned periodically to Secret Service offices in the United States or a on a foreign liaison assignment in a different country.

If you can make it through the tough screening process and get hired, you'll be employed by the U.S. Secret Service, which is part of the Department of Homeland Security. If you're ready to apply for a special agent job, make sure that you meet the requirements described above. Then submit a typewritten Standard Form 171, Application for Federal Employment. If you have completed college, you will also need to submit an official transcript. Alternatively, you can submit an Optional Application for Federal Employment or a résumé, but you'll have to complete some accompanying forms, so be sure to check with the Secret Service field office nearest you to find out exactly what forms to fill out. The field office in your area should be listed in the government section of your telephone book.

To find out what vacancies currently exist with the Secret Service, call its personnel division at 202-406-5271 or go online at http://www.secretservice.gov/opportunities.shtml.

WHERE CAN I GO FROM HERE?

Norm began working in the Secret Service's Salt Lake City field office in 1984. He was transferred to the Organized Crime Task Force in the Washington, D. C., field office in 1987. In 1990 Norm was promoted to the position of instructor at the Office of Training, and he was transferred to the Presidential Protective Division in 1994. Norm ended up in Montana in 1997 after being promoted to the position of resident agent of the Great Falls field office.

Generally, special agents begin their career by spending 7 to 10 years performing primarily investigative duties at a field office. Then they are usually assigned to a protective assignment for 3 to 5 years. After 12 or 13 years, special agents become eligible to move into a supervisory position. A typical promotion path moves special agents to the position of senior agent, then resident agent in charge of a district, assistant to the special agent in charge, and finally special agent in charge of a field office or headquarters division. Since the Secret Service employs many highly skilled professionals, promotions are very competitive and are awarded based on performance.

Special agents can retire after completing 25 years of service and after reaching age 50. Special agents must retire before the age of 57.

Some retired agents get hired to organize logistics for corporations needing to move either people or products from one place to another. Other agents work as bodyguards, private investigators, security consultants, and local law enforcement officials.

WHAT ARE THE SALARY RANGES?

Special agents generally receive law enforcement availability pay on top of their base pay. Agents usually start at the GS-5, GS-7, or GS-9 grade levels, which were $24,677, $30,567, and $37,390 in 2004, respectively, plus Law Enforcement Availability Pay (25 percent of their base salary). Salaries may be slightly higher in some areas with high costs of living. Agents automatically advance by two pay grades each year, until they reach the GS-12 level, which was $54,221 in 2004. Agents must compete for positions above the GS-12 level; however, the majority of agents become a GS-13—$64,478 in 2004—in their career. Top officials in the Secret Service are appointed to Senior Executive Service (SES) positions, which are exempt from the availability pay. Senior Executive Service salaries ranged from $104,927 to $158,100 in 2004.

Benefits for special agents include low-cost health and life insurance; annual vacation and sick leave; paid holidays; a comprehensive retirement program. In addition, free financial

Related Jobs

- air marshals
- border patrol agents
- deputy sheriffs
- detectives
- FBI agents
- fingerprint classifiers
- fire wardens
- fish and game wardens
- narcotics investigators
- police officers
- private investigators
- state highway patrol officers
- U.S. marshals

protection is provided to agents and their families in the event of job-related injury or death.

WHAT IS THE JOB OUTLOOK?

Compared to other federal law enforcement agencies, the Secret Service is small. It employs about 6,400 people, 3,200 of whom are special agents. As a result, the number of agents it hires each year is limited. Individuals with prior experience in law enforcement and advanced degrees will have the best employment prospects.

SECTION 3

Do It Yourself

If you've made it this far through the book, it's probably because a career in safety and security is starting to sound like a definite possibility. You're committed to serving your community and, even after reading the career profiles, you aren't discouraged by the dangers and difficulties experienced by virtually everyone in this field. Chances are that if you're this interested in working for the public safety now, you'd rather not wait until high school graduation to start working toward your chosen career. The good news—which you may have guessed from the title of the book—is that you don't have to.

It's true that there aren't as many established ways for teenagers to prepare for safety- and security-related careers as there are to prepare for careers in, say, the environment. In that field, there are any number of universities offering precollege courses for high school students; and state parks, animal sanctuaries, and activist groups offering internship and employment opportunities. You're unlikely to find many comparable opportunities in public safety, mainly because of state and local regulations on the age and amount of training required for those working in the field.

This may seem a trifle unfair, especially if your community has particularly strict regulations. But the life and safety of people and property are on the line in this industry and must be safeguarded by every possible means. You surely know from personal experience that some people under the age of 18—or even 21—are just not mature or responsible enough to work in public safety. On the other hand, some young people do have the capability and commitment to start actively pursuing careers from firefighting to the Secret Service. And if you are one of those people, there are things you can do right now.

Preparing for a career in safety and security can entail a fairly broad range of activities, many of which are listed in this section. The ones you choose will depend on how certain you are of your career choice, how much time you can and will devote now to career preparation, and which options are available or practicable in your community. Some activities are directly linked to specific careers, to the point where you are effectively a police cadet or junior firefighter. Others involve you with people working in the field or expose you to the work they do. Still other activities help you acquire the kinds of skills and characteristics needed in public safety jobs. We don't endorse any particular organizations or activities, but we do encourage you to research and explore them for yourself.

❏ THE DIRECT ROUTE TO SAFETY AND SECURITY CAREERS

If you think you're ready to make a serious career commitment—or at the very least a serious time commitment—then this is the section for you. Many of the programs here demand several hours of your free time, meaning the time you now spend on studying, socializing, working at a paying job, or pursuing other extra-

By the Way

Throughout this section, we offer suggestions on who to contact to get involved with the public safety programs on offer. Usually, the contact is the EMS, fire, or police department in your own neighborhood; occasionally, we give you the name and address of a national organization. But when you're ready to contact someone, what should you actually do?

If you want to speak with one of the public safety services in your community, do not call 911! That number is exclusively for emergencies. Instead, look in the telephone book: either the inside front cover or the blue "Government" pages will give you the regular business phone numbers you need. If you know for certain that they have a program you want to join (perhaps Explorers or the Police Athletic/Activities League), simply ask to speak to the person in charge of that program. If you're not after a specific program or are not sure what they offer, just explain who you are and why you are calling. It's a good idea to write this out before getting on the telephone. That makes things clear in your own mind and ensures that you don't confuse or waste the time of the person who answers your call.

Once you figure out exactly whom you need to speak with, you may well find that he or she is out on the job. Leave your name, telephone number, and a brief message about the reason for your call, asking the person to call you back. If your call is not returned in a few days, try again! Be persistent until you make personal contact; after all, it's your future we're talking about. When you finally do make contact, be very clear and direct about what you're interested in. Again, it can really help to write up a few sentences beforehand, and you may also want to note any pressing questions you would like answered.

If you're contacting a national organization, it's again important to be very specific about what you hope to get: more information, the address of a local branch, an application packet, etc. Your request may be complex enough to warrant a carefully written letter or e-mail instead of a phone call; use your own judgment, and remember that writing things out really helps to clarify them.

Finally, no matter who you are calling or writing, always do it yourself. Don't let mom or dad do it for you. If you want to prepare for your adult life, if you want to take charge of your future, start now. If you want to get involved, you have to get in touch.

---

curricular activities. Some are connected to your high school curriculum, others are concerned with your college career—including your summer breaks and post-graduation plans.

These kinds of commitments are always a bit intimidating, but the rewards they bring can be amazing. If you're interested in an intelligence career, some of the programs listed here can guarantee an intelligence job waiting for you as soon as you complete your college degree. If you're pursuing a vo-tech program in law enforcement now, joining the Law

Enforcement Explorers can lead you toward national recognition in your field. If you want to be a firefighter, the Fire Fighting Explorers program can have you working in a fire station before you even finish high school.

If you're serious about a career in safety and security, the following resources will helping you make it happen.

BSA Explorers

BSA stands for Boy Scouts of America, but if you're female, don't let that stop you from reading this section! The BSA Explorers program is for everybody—it just happens to have been started by the Boy Scouts. They believe, as you do, that when hands-on career experience is available to people still in their teens, it makes them especially well prepared to enter the world of work after graduation from high school or college. So they've developed the Explorers program for young people between the ages of 14 and 20. Groups of young people—sometimes from established Boy Scout troops, sometimes not—with a common interest in a specific career form their own Explorer posts to pursue that interest. And what are some of the most popular careers for exploration? Law enforcement, firefighting, and emergency medical services.

Explorer posts in these career areas are actually part of their communities' regular public safety services. For example, law enforcement Explorer posts are part of their cities' or townships' police departments. Student members of the posts are guided by adult leaders (e.g., an actual police officer or firefighter), but

are themselves responsible for planning activities and ensuring that the post functions as it should. Democracy is the guiding principle of each Explorer post, and activities are carried out in a completely voluntary, supportive, and adventurous environment.

All Explorers must subscribe to a code of convictions and duties and, as part of their post, work on goals and activities addressing career, leadership, fitness, social, service, and outdoor concerns. Each post also establishes membership and organization rules and a code of conduct designed to protect both the Explorers and the community they serve. Young people must live up to their responsibilities in the Explorer post or face not attaining or losing full membership.

Law Enforcement Explorers

Law enforcement is an exceedingly popular Explorer post specialty endorsed by such organizations as the International Association of Chiefs of Police and the National Sheriffs' Association. Fortunately, there are more than 3,000 law enforcement Explorer posts around the country, so you just might find one in your area.

Explorers in these posts assist police officers in such matters as crime prevention, traffic control, and facilitating community events. Some Explorers participate in the Ride-Along Program, which entails accompanying police officers on their patrols. These Explorers experience the job firsthand and assist their officers when someone in the community calls for help. Special care is taken not to involve students riding along in dangerous situations such as shoot-outs.

It is important to remember that, although Explorers take on important policing responsibilities, work with police officers, and wear modified police uniforms, they are not police officers. They must never pretend to be (that's impersonating a police officer, and it's a crime!), and they must never place themselves in a situation where a trained professional is required.

If you are interested in joining or setting up a law enforcement Explorer post, contact your local police department or Learning for Life, which "provides training and support for Explorer posts through a nationwide network of over 300 local offices."

Learning for Life
1325 West Walnut Hill Lane, PO
    Box 152079
Irving, TX 75015-2079
972-580-2433
http://www.learningforlife.org/
    exploring/lawenforcement/index.
    html

Firefighting Explorers

Although many states and cities bar young people from actually fighting fires, those who are members of Explorer posts are able to help their local fire departments maintain their equipment, assist in drills, and perform support tasks when a fire is being fought. Again depending on local rules and regulations, some Explorers are able to fight small brush fires, that do not threaten lives or property.

Naturally, personal safety has to be a top priority for firefighters; you're sure to learn safety techniques and precautionary measures from working with the professionals, even if you never get to fight a single fire while in the Explorers. You'll also gain an understanding and appreciation of teamwork when you witness and experience the trust firefighters put in each other.

If you are interested in starting or joining such a program, contact your community's fire department or Learning for Life.

Learning for Life
1325 West Walnut Hill Lane, PO
    Box 152079
Irving, TX 75015-2079
972-580-2433
http://www.learningforlife.org/
    exploring/fire/index.html

Emergency Medical Services Explorers

Explorer posts with this specialty can be quite difficult to locate, largely due to the huge responsibilities of EMS and the medical training needed to undertake them. There are also logistical problems: administering medications may be age restricted, driving the ambulance is generally not for teenagers, and rescue squads often have no room for anyone but the patient and one or two EMTs.

Despite all this, some Explorer posts are still able to specialize in emergency medical services. Explorers in these posts help the EMTs maintain their medical equipment and keep the ambulance in a state of readiness. They may ride to emergency situations in a special car ahead of or behind the rescue squad and perform basic support tasks at the scene. Explorers sometimes help out when the EMS runs blood pressure checks or cholesterol screenings for the community.

You'll need to get in touch with your community's own emergency medical services (possibly affiliated with the fire department) to see if they have an Explorer post or are interested in setting up one. Or, contact Learning for Life, which has information on local programs.

Learning for Life
1325 West Walnut Hill Lane, PO
    Box 152079
Irving, TX 75015-2079
972-580-2433
http://www.learningforlife.org/
    exploring/health/index.html

Starting Your Own Explorer Post

As we've said, the simplest and most direct way to get involved with the Explorers program is to contact Learning for Life or your local police, fire, or EMS department and see if there is already an Explorer post for you to join. Sometimes, however, there may not be one. Don't let that discourage you from getting involved; think of this situation as an opportunity to start your own post and take a leadership role in running it.

If, when you contact the public safety service that interests you, you find that it does not have an affiliated Explorer post, ask if any other young people have expressed an interest in Explorers. Inquire, too, as to whether any specific officers (or firefighters or EMTs) have shown an interest in Explorers and whether the department as a whole is interested in the program. It is important to do both of these things because you must have potential student members and potential adult leaders to start an Explorer post.

If you find a lack of interest on one end, don't give up immediately. Your high school may provide a number of potential members if you orchestrate a publicity campaign carefully explaining the Explorers program and the career you wish to explore as a post. This can be done via your school newspaper, posters, leaflets, announcements, and word of mouth. On the other hand, if you know a few other potential members, you can all prepare a letter or presentation about the Explorers program and your career goals for the public safety department concerned. With a better understanding of what's involved, the department may be more inclined to form a post.

Ultimately, you may find that an Explorers program is just not an option in your community. The lack of interest may be too serious a problem, or you may find your efforts hampered by those infamous state and local age requirements. But don't let your new contacts in the police, fire, or EMS departments go to waste! Ask them about other programs you might be able to join and other suggestions about what you can do right now. And read on for still more ideas.

❑ TRAINING FOR INTELLIGENCE CAREERS

While some of the programs that follow are aimed at graduating seniors who want to kick-start their postsecondary careers, others are for teenagers who hope to work in intelligence now. You won't be sent to exotic locales or entrusted with secrets vital to national security, but you will be serving the government—and you might be embarking on a promising career.

The Central Intelligence Agency

The Central Intelligence Agency (CIA) has developed its Undergraduate Scholar Program for minority and disabled high school seniors (although the program is open to everyone) planning to enter a four- or five-year college program. (Students already in their sophomore year are also eligible.) Those accepted into the program become part of America's foreign intelligence effort by working for the CIA full time every summer of their undergraduate career. Transportation to and from Washington, D.C., is provided along with a housing allowance. Participants receive a salary, college tuition up to $18,000 annually, and a full-time position with the agency upon graduation from college.

To qualify, you must be a U.S. citizen, 18 years of age by April 1 of your senior year, and in need of financial assistance for college tuition. Furthermore, you must have a GPA of 3.0 or higher (on a 4.0 scale) and SAT scores of at least 1000 or ACT scores of at least 21. While taking part in the program, you must maintain a GPA of 2.75 or higher in college and meet the same performance standards as CIA employees in comparable positions.

Needless to say, this opportunity in foreign intelligence is highly desirable and therefore very competitive. For you to be considered, the CIA must receive your cover letter, résumé, and a copy of your current high school transcript with standardized test scores by November 1 of your senior year. There is no application form. Visit the program's Web site for more information.

CIA Undergraduate Scholar Program

http://www.odci.gov/employment/jobs/students_scholar.html

The Federal Bureau of Investigation

The Federal Bureau of Investigation (FBI) offers its ten-week Volunteer Internship Program to highly motivated high school, college, and graduate students. Interns learn about a variety of careers within the FBI while working alongside special agents and other staff. For quaiification and application information, visit the Web site below.

FBI Volunteer Internship Program

http://www.fbijobs.gov/239.asp#4

The U.S. Department of State

The U.S. Department of State offers several opportunities for promising high school students to explore and pursue careers in foreign policy and international relations. Competition is tight, so apply as far in advance of your expected start date as possible.

In its Summer Clerical Program, young people work in office support positions in which they gain work experience and a better understanding of the inner workings of the State Department. Participants work during the summer and over the holidays. To be eligible for this program, you must be a U.S. citizen, be 16 years of age or older at the time of appointment, be enrolled or accepted for enrollment in a postsecondary program, and pass a background check. Applications are due by February 1 in the year in which you wish to begin work. For more information, contact the State Department.

U.S. Department of State
Attn: Summer Clerical Program
   Coordinator
Recruitment Division, SA-1
2401 E Street NW, Suite 518H
Washington, DC 20522-0001
http://www.careers.state.gov/student/
   programs/summer_clerical.html

The Stay-in-School Program is designed for students who require financial assistance to continue their education. In this program, you may work in technical, clerical, or administrative positions part time during the school year or full time during the holidays and summer vacation. To be eligible for this program, you must be a U.S. citizen, pass a background check, and be enrolled in a high school, vocational, or undergraduate program. Contact your guidance counselor or state employment service to learn more about the financial criteria. For more information, contact the State Department.

U.S. Department of State
Attn: Stay-in-School Program
   Coordinator
Recruitment Division, SA-1
2401 E Street NW, Suite 518H
Washington, DC 20522-0001
http://www.careers.state.gov/student/
   programs/stay_in_school.html

Finally, the State Department offers a Cooperative Education Program, which integrates and coordinates academic studies with on-the-job experience. To be eligible for this program, you must be a U.S. citizen, be in good academic standing, be enrolled in your school's cooperative education program, and pass a background check. Co-op opportunities are available from high school through graduate school; contact your school co-op coordinator (probably your guidance counselor) for more details. For more information, contact the State Department.

U.S. Department of State
Attn: Cooperative Program
   Coordinator
Recruitment Division, SA-1
2401 E Street NW, Suite 518H
Washington, DC 20522-0001
http://www.careers.state.gov/
   student/programs/coop_edu.html

❏ MEETING THE PEOPLE AND LEARNING THE WORK

This section offers a number of career exploration and preparation opportunities covering most of the public safety field. These activities don't represent career paths as direct as those in the last section, where participants could be associates of a fire department or guarantee themselves a job with the CIA. What's listed in this section are suggestions for getting to know people already working in public safety and experiencing the kinds of duties they perform on a daily basis.

These kinds of activities can be useful to you no matter what your personal situation. If you're confident about your career choice, they'll allow you to learn firsthand about the job you'll be doing as an adult and about the people you'll be working with. If you're still unsure about your career choice, these activities will allow you to make a more informed decision, without requiring the dedication and time commitments of programs like Explorers.

You can be involved in more than one of these activities, and you have some flexibility in deciding when and how often you will participate. At least some of the activities listed here are available in almost every community around the country. And as always, you can use the suggestions here to form ideas and activities of your own, creating opportunities tailored to your interests and your community's needs.

Emergency Medical Services

It can be difficult to get hands-on experience for a career as an emergency medical technician or paramedic because the age and certification requirements in this field tend to be especially strict. However, virtually every community offers high school students the opportunity to work with health care professionals and learn how to care for the sick and injured.

Medical Volunteer Work

Though often associated with preparation for careers in nursing, volunteering at a hospital (or "candystriping," as it is often called) is fantastic preparation for careers in emergency medical services. Almost all hospitals—public and private, general, children's, and veterans'—use volunteers to perform routine health care tasks. This not only gives them a chance to explore medical careers, it also gives the nurses and doctors more time to perform complicated and specialized tasks.

Because this kind of volunteer work is so common, it will be easy for you to get started. Simply call the hospital where you would like to work and tell the receptionist who answers that you are interested in volunteering; your call will then be forwarded to a volunteer coordinator or a volunteer association. The person in charge of the volunteer program will tell you the age and other requirements (generally, you must be at least 13 or 14) and will explain the training procedures.

Training procedures vary widely, but a few generalizations can be made. You may train either one-on-one with a nurse or volunteer coordinator, or in a group with other new volunteers. You're likely to train one-on-one if you start during the school year and in a group if your volunteering is part of a summer program. The training may last a couple of hours or a couple of days, depending on the size and scope of the hospital's operations and on the duties you will be expected to perform.

In general, you can expect to learn how to feed patients, take temperatures, assist patients who have difficulty walking, run errands between wards, and get supplies. If you are to work in a pediatrics ward, you will learn special child care skills. Once you are trained, you and the volunteer coordinator will work out a regular schedule and you can then get to work! Not only will your health care skills be put to the test, but you will also see just how well you cope with people who are unwell and need all your patience and compassion.

In addition to hospitals, you can usually find similar volunteer positions at nursing homes and hospices. You might also want to seek formal instruction in caring for the sick and injured by taking a CPR or first aid class; details are listed in "Gaining Skills and Strengths," which appears later in this chapter.

Firefighting

Firefighting is such a dangerous job that comparatively few communities allow young people to take an active part in it. But like most people working for the public safety, firefighters find their work rewarding and are happy to encourage young people to consider it as a career. Your local fire department, whether volunteer or professional, may have a program that gets teenagers involved with the firefighters. Or, you may be able to arrange a tour of the fire station for yourself or your class. Call your fire department and tell them of your interest.

Teaching Fire Safety to Others

It's likely that when you were a small child, a local firefighter—or even a whole fire engine crew—came to your elementary school to teach you about fire safety.

That's where you learned the famous stop-drop-and-roll fire extinguishing technique! Could you now help your fire department put on its fire safety presentations? Could you help them show a video, distribute pamphlets to the students, assist in their demonstrations of stop-drop-and-roll? This would involve getting permission to miss a couple of your own classes, but it certainly would be a great opportunity to meet the firefighters and share fire safety tips with others. Call your local fire department to discuss the possibility.

If the department welcomes your help, you might also want to consider jointly planning fire safety presentations for junior and senior high school students. You know what people in these age groups find interesting, and you could suggest creative ways of presenting basic safety guidelines. These ideas—and the concept of a high school student being involved with the presentation—might be new to your fire department, but if you demonstrate your sincere interest in public safety, the firefighters are likely to at least consider them.

Fire Drills and Escape Plans

You might also be able to work with your fire department and your school on the fire drills and fire escape plans set up for you and your classmates. These elements are crucial to everyone's safety, but they are often a bit mysterious. How are fire drills organized? How often are they held? How are fire escape plans made? When are they revised or reviewed? How thoroughly are escape procedures explained to students and teachers? How often are fire alarms and extinguishers checked for problems? And who's in charge of all this? If your principal or a firefighter can take the time to answer all these questions, you'll have received a real education!

But you may be able to do more than ask questions. Once you've found out who's in charge, find out if that person needs an assistant—and volunteer for the job! You'll learn more about fire safety while actually helping to protect others. If your school's administration just isn't ready to take you on as an assistant, remember that it's because their top concern is also public safety. They may be following state safety guidelines, they may want to have just one person bear the responsibility, or they may simply want only adults involved.

Law Enforcement

Getting to know your local police department is a vital part of public safety in general and of your career preparations in particular. Various community programs allow you to develop friendly relationships with police officers and act as their eyes and ears when they can't be around in person. Your purpose in such programs is to prevent crimes from occurring and to solve them once they do. You therefore share the same goals as police officers and, in a limited way, also share their work.

Bicycle Registration and Safety

This isn't a glamorous crime-fighting activity, but it is a great way to assist your local police department and contribute to public safety. In many, if not most, com- munities, the police register the bicycles of young children so that they can be identified in case of theft or accident. Police are also often responsible for pre- sentations and brochures that teach kids about bicycle safety, particularly riding bicycles alongside automobile traffic. If your local law enforcement agency does this kind of work, why not volunteer to help? On a bicycle registration day, you might help with record-keeping, direct- ing children to the right areas, distribut- ing literature, or assisting the officers on duty. If officers are planning presenta- tions at local malls or schools, you might assist there, too. Simply contact your police department.

Neighborhood Watch and Community Policing

These are two programs that will not only keep you in touch with your local police department, but that will also make the area where you live a safer place. Neigh- borhood Watch is a well-established program in which community residents are trained to recognize and report sus- picious activities before actual crimes are committed. Of course, they also report crimes that are in progress or completed, but the ideal is to alert police before vio- lence and damage is done and while the suspects are still on the scene.

The success of the program hinges on the cooperation between local law enforcement and the community. The volunteer neighborhood coordinator is assisted by a number of volunteer block captains, while all of the block watchers agree to look out for the safety of their neighbors. Block captains host Neighborhood Watch meetings, often monthly, which bring together their block watchers and liaisons from the police department. The law enforcement officers provide all Neighborhood Watch participants with literature and other information on identifying suspicious activities and making their homes and valuables more secure.

If your community has a Neighborhood Watch program, it's well worth getting involved. Try to join the program with your entire household, so that you are all trained and ready to act for the public safety. If there is no Neighborhood Watch in your community, contact the police department to see about starting one; it doesn't take very much money or time to run the program, and there are many model programs around the country that can give you ideas and tips on getting started. Check with the cities located near you.

Community policing is a relatively new program that may mean different things in different police departments. The common thread that runs through most community policing programs is the close interaction of members of the community (that means you, your parents, and your friends) with members of the law enforcement community. The goal is to acquaint the officer and neighborhood residents with each other, developing a sense of trust and friendship, and to alert police (in the same manner as the Neighborhood Watch program) to suspicious activities before they evolve into crimes or to work together to help avoid crime in the future. If community policing has been introduced in your area, get to know your patrol officers by attend-

ing community policing meetings, and do your part to keep them informed about what's going on in the neighborhood. This could be an opportunity to develop a special friendship with one such law enforcement officer.

Police Athletic/Activities Leagues (PALs)

If you're really interested in meeting police officers, find out if your community has a Police Athletic/Activities League. Instead of sitting around the house with your friends, you can all be outside playing football or basketball with your town's own law enforcement officers! PALs keep young people busy and encourage them to take police officers as their role models. This means that you'll have the opportunity to find out what it's really like to work in law enforcement from the people who know.

If you take your sports almost as seriously as you take public safety, you'll feel right at home with the Police Athletic/Activities Leagues. They sponsor competitions at the regional and state level, so you can really work on your game—whatever it is. The National Association of Police Athletic/Activities Leagues even sponsors national tournaments in selected sports. Girls are welcome in PALs.

National Association of Police Athletic/Activities Leagues
658 West Indiantown Road, #201
Jupiter, FL 33458-7535
561-745-5535
copnkid@nationalpal.org
http://www.nationalpal.org

Scholastic Crime Stoppers

You've probably heard of Crime Stoppers International, which focuses on unsolved crimes and asks ordinary citizens to anonymously phone in tips and leads, with reward money available if a conviction is secured. Scholastic Crime Stoppers is a student branch of that organization, focusing primarily on high schools. Members of Scholastic Crime Stoppers work with school administrators to set up and run a similar anonymous-tip-and-reward program within their high schools. They send a clear message: teenagers will not tolerate crime.

Of course, that's just the kind of message you want to send—so consider getting involved with your school's Scholastic Crime Stoppers program or starting one of your own. Students run the program's board of directors at their school, reviewing information about crimes already committed, raising and allotting reward money, and publicizing the program among their peers. The names of victims, witnesses, and suspects are known only to school administrators, and not to boards of directors. From hotlines to video reenactments, Scholastic Crime Stoppers groups use every method their creativity can devise to accomplish their goals. You can get involved, take on a leadership or supporting role, and make your school a safer place.

If your school doesn't already have a Scholastic Crime Stoppers group, contact the U.S. branch of Crime Stoppers International for information about starting one.

Crime Stoppers USA
info.csusa@crimestopusa.com
http://www.crimestopusa.com

❏ GAINING SKILLS AND STRENGTHS

If you are still having trouble finding ways to prepare for a career in safety and security, or if you feel the other preparations you're making just aren't enough, there are still more activities you should consider—and they're available almost everywhere. Best of all, the skills and strengths taught and improved by the listings below will be useful to you no matter what career you finally choose. So, even if you feel that something like Explorers is too much of a commitment to careers in safety and security, you can plunge into these activities fearlessly!

Taking Classes

You may not be very enthusiastic about taking even more classes than your high school requires, but doing so can put you at a real advantage in the years to come. Actually, many of the courses suggested here are probably offered by your school, so you can gain credit for them and not take on an extra commitment. Or you may have the chance to take these classes at a local college, public library, or community center—all of which can be great new opportunities for you.

Academics and Athletics

Computers have long been used by state and federal public safety agencies, but today, even some of the smallest municipal police departments and fire stations are using them in their work. Since you can expect to use computers in at least some aspects of your future career (chiefly record-keeping and correspondence, but also in more complex capacities if you work as a crime analyst or in an intelligence career), why not learn to use them now? Basic typing and word processing skills, simple Internet navigation, and the use of databases to store information are important skills in this and almost every field. Your school probably offers some computer classes, but if not, they are likely offered by a local library, college, or community center. And if you get beyond the basics, you'll be at a real advantage when applying to colleges or employers.

For most safety and security careers, the knowledge of a foreign language is a real asset—and depending on exactly what kind of job you want, it may be a requirement. After all, won't a basic command of Spanish make you a more effective border patrol guard? And is the State Department likely to send you on an exciting overseas assignment if you can't converse with the locals or read the newspapers? Fortunately, your school almost certainly offers foreign language classes you can take now. If you're particularly interested in a language not offered in school, your public library or local community college should be able to give you some leads, even if they don't offer classes themselves.

Common sense—and the career articles earlier in the book—make it clear that most people working in safety and security must have achieved a considerable degree of physical fitness. No, you

don't have to be a star athlete, but you must be agile and quick enough to carry out your duties and not needlessly endanger your own safety. You can get a jump on the exercise and fitness requirements that you're certain to encounter later by becoming more active now. It can be as simple as walking or jogging regularly in a nearby park, swimming twice a week at the YMCA, or joining an intramural sport at school. Consult a professional organization or Web site connected to the career that interests you to get some specifics on the fitness requirements.

Please note that people with physical disabilities are not barred from pursuing careers in safety and security. If you are concerned about certain duties performed in a specific job like EMT or Secret Service agent, discuss the situation with a related professional organization or your own guidance counselor.

First Aid and Beyond

Regardless of which public safety career interests you, you should seriously consider taking a class in first aid or CPR—or both. Your local Red Cross, YMCA, or hospital most likely offers this kind of training for a reasonable fee. CPR and first aid skills are of vital importance to every law enforcement officer, firefighter, and, of course, emergency medical technician, and you can get a head start. But before you actually begin your career—and even if you eventually decide not to go into public safety at all—CPR and first aid courses will allow you to react promptly and effectively to any medical emergency. How should you react if a teacher faints in class? What should you do if a class-mate cuts herself badly in industrial arts? If you've taken the proper courses, you'll know.

Besides first aid and CPR, the Red Cross offers a number of courses and programs that are worth exploring. After all, what single organization does more for public safety than they do? They can provide you with the training needed to educate your peers and your community about HIV/AIDS, staying healthy, swim-ming and water safety, and responding to disasters. Each local Red Cross office has different programs available, so call the one nearest you to see what it offers for teenagers. Visit the American Red Cross's extensive Web site for help in locating an office in your area.

American Red Cross
2025 E Street NW
Washington, DC 20006-5009
202-303-4498
http://www.redcross.org

❏ BUILDING CHARACTER

If there's one thing that sounds less appeal-ing than taking extra classes, it's probably building character! That's because build-ing character has a bad rap; you prob-ably associate it with all the chores and responsibilities that you don't like to do. But character building is no bad thing; you've probably found for yourself that confronting new and challenging situ-ations makes you a stronger and more capable person. And the bottom line is that no one is more in demand in the field

of safety and security than the strong and capable person.

As important as skills and work expe-rience are, your character is paramount in establishing how effective you will be as a worker in this field, and it is likely to considerably influence what kind of employer will hire you. Safety and secu-rity organizations can teach you how to hold a fire hose or analyze fingerprints, for example, but only you can determine the quality of your character. Intelligence agencies in particular demand evidence of their employees' good character—and that goes well beyond not having a crimi-nal record. So what kind of evidence can you offer? The activities you pursue in your free time speak volumes about your character.

Since every safety and security career is one of service to the community, the best way to spend at least some of your free time is in service to others. But this doesn't have to mean drudgery or unful-filling work. On the contrary, there are so many service options that you are certain to find a job you'll enjoy almost as much as the people you're helping appreciate your work!

❏ SERVING THE COMMUNITY

One of the first community service options that comes to mind is working with the less fortunate: the poor, the sick, the neglected. Your city's department of health and human services, your school system, and your church, temple, or mosque are all likely to run programs to help these people—and they're all likely to welcome your involvement. It may take only a few hours a week or one Saturday a month to collect clothes for needy children, take food to the homebound elderly, or mow the lawn for a person who has difficulty walking. And if you can't find a service program that appeals to you, or if you see a need for a program that doesn't yet exist, work with one of the institutions listed above and start your own. That shows initiative and character!

Other ways to build character through public service include working to improve the environment and supporting charitable organizations. You don't have to take on environmental issues of global proportions like the greenhouse effect or rainforest destruction—although you're certainly welcome to do so! But in your own community, whether it's large or small, there are recycling issues, pollution problems, and threatened habitats that need your help. You may choose to work with an established environmental group or on your own as a concerned citizen. Either way, you are performing a valuable service for all your neighbors—and all those of the future.

Charitable organizations are, of course, often an intrinsic part of helping the less fortunate and working for environmental protection. However, you can be of service to any number of charities concerned with other community issues: education, religious and political causes,

the fine arts, science, history, sports, and many more. Your involvement doesn't have to involve financial contributions at all: the donation of your time is most valuable to the charities and to your career goals.

All of these contributions to the world around you demonstrate your interest in and commitment to people and values besides yourself. And, sure enough, the new situations and challenges you'll encounter in these activities will build up your character! Your involvement shows your good character and your commitment to public service to colleges and employers more clearly than any application form or essay ever could.

❏ FINALLY . . .

Regardless of which safety and security activities you're able to become involved with right now, make sure you're doing something. Your interest in this career field is important because the tasks done by workers in this field are so vital, and good workers are so essential. That's obviously true of policing and firefighting, but it is equally true of lower-profile jobs in corrections and intelligence. Should your career exploration prove that safety and security isn't the right field for you, you will nevertheless have gained new friends, new skills, and a new appreciation of the men and women who keep us safe and secure.

SECTION 4

What Can I Do Right Now?

Get Involved: A Directory of Camps, Programs, and Competitions

Now that you've read about some of the different careers available in safety and security, you may be anxious to experience this line of work for yourself, to find out what it's really like. Or perhaps you already feel certain that this is the career path for you and want to get started on it right away. Whichever is the case, this section is for you! While the often dangerous and sometimes secretive nature of careers in this field may limit the opportunities available to students, there are still things you can do right now to learn about public safety careers while gaining valuable experience. Just as important, you'll get to meet new friends and see new places, too.

In the following pages you will find programs designed to pique your interest in safety and security and to start preparing you for a career. You already know that this field is demanding and often dangerous and that to work in it you need a solid education. Since the first step toward a public safety career will be gaining that education, we've found more than 15 programs that will start you on your way. Some are special introductory sessions, others are actual college courses—one of them may be right for you. Take time to read over the listings and see how each compares to your situation: how committed you are to public safety, how much of your money and free time you're willing to devote to it, and how the program will help you after high school. These listings are divided into categories, with the type of program printed right after its name or the name of the sponsoring organization.

❏ THE CATEGORIES

Camps

When you see an activity that is classified as a camp, don't automatically start packing your tent and mosquito repellent. Where academic study is involved, the term "camp" often simply means a residential program including both educational and recreational activities. It's sometimes hard to differentiate between such camps and other study programs, but if the sponsoring organization calls it a camp, so do we!

College Courses/Summer Study

These terms are linked because most college courses offered to students your age must take place in the summer, when you are out of school. At the same time, many summer study programs are sponsored by colleges and universities that want to attract future students and give them a head start in higher education. Summer study of almost any type is a good idea because it keeps your mind and your study skills sharp over the long vacation. Summer study at a college offers any number of additional benefits, including giving you the tools to make a well-informed decision about your future academic career.

Competitions

Competitions are fairly self explanatory, but you should know that there are only a few in this book for the following reason: many public safety competitions (most typically first aid competitions) are at the local and regional levels and are impractical to list here. What this means, however, is that if you are interested in entering a competition, you shouldn't have much trouble finding one yourself. Your guidance counselor or health teacher can help you start searching in your area.

Conferences

Conferences for high school students are usually difficult to track down because most are for professionals in the field who gather to share new information and ideas with each other. Don't be discouraged, though. A number of professional organizations with student branches invite those student members to their conferences and plan special events for them. Some student branches even run their own conferences; check the directory of organizations at the end of this section for possible leads. This is an option worth pursuing because conferences focus on some of the most current information available and also give you the chance to meet professionals who can answer your questions and even offer advice.

Employment and Internship Opportunities

As you may already know from experience, employment opportunities for teenagers—especially in safety and security—can be very limited. Securing the safety of the public is a huge responsibility, and as a young person, you do not yet have the experience or the education to work in occupations such as police work, firefighting, or intelligence gathering. That experience and training will come in time, so remain positive and look for opportunities that will give you at least a glimpse of life in the field of your choice. Some organizations, such as the Central Intelligence Agency (CIA), hire high school and college students to do clerical work during their summer vacations and holiday breaks. Consider applying for employment at the CIA or other government agencies listed in this section, or contact your local police, fire, and emergency services departments to see if they have set up similar programs.

Field Experience

This is something of a catchall category for activities that don't exactly fit the other descriptions. But anything called a field experience in this book is always a good opportunity to get out and explore the work of safety and security professionals.

Membership

When an organization is in this category, it simply means that you are welcome to pay your dues and become a card-carrying member. Formally joining any organization brings the benefits of meeting others who share your interests, finding opportunities to get involved, and keeping up with current events. Depending on how active you are, the contacts you make and the experiences you gain may help when the time comes to apply to colleges or look for a job.

In some organizations, you pay a special student rate and receive benefits similar to regular members. Many organizations, however, are now starting student branches with their own benefits and publications. As in any field, make sure you understand exactly what the benefits of membership are before you join.

Finally, don't let membership dues discourage you from making contact with these organizations. Some charge dues as low as $10 because they know that students are perpetually short of funds. When the annual dues are higher, think of the money as an investment in your future and then consider if it is too much to pay.

❏ PROGRAM DESCRIPTIONS

Once you've started to look at the individual listings, you'll find that they contain a lot of information. Naturally, there is a general description of each program, but wherever possible we also have included the following details.

Application Information

Once you have determined the application deadline for participating in a specific opportunity, apply for the program or position as far in advance as possible.

This ensures that you won't miss out on a great opportunity simply because other people got there ahead of you. It also means that you will get a timely decision on your application, so if you are not accepted, you'll still have some time to apply elsewhere. As for the things that make up your application—essays, recommendations, etc.—we've tried to tell you what's involved, but be sure to contact the program about specific requirements before you submit anything.

Background Information

This includes such information as the date, the name of the organization that is sponsoring it financially, and the faculty and staff who will be there for you. This can help you—and your family—gauge the quality and reliability of the program.

Classes and Activities

Classes and activities change from year to year, depending on popularity, the availability of instructors, and many other factors. Nevertheless, colleges and universities quite consistently offer the same or similar classes, even in their summer sessions. Courses like Introduction to Criminal Justice and Forensics 101, for example, are simply indispensable. So you can look through the listings and see which programs offer foundational courses like these and which offer courses on more variable topics. As for activities, we note when you have access to recreational facilities on campus, and it's usually a given that special social and cultural activities will be arranged for these programs.

Contact Information

Wherever possible, we have given the title of the person whom you should contact instead of the name because people change jobs so frequently. If no title is given and you are telephoning an organization, simply tell the person who answers the phone the name of the program that interests you and he or she will forward your call. If you are writing, include the line "Attention: Summer Study Program" or "Attn: Summer Study Program" (or whatever is appropriate after "Attention") somewhere on the envelope. This will help to ensure that your letter goes to the person in charge of that program.

Credit

Where academic programs are concerned, we sometimes note that high school or college credit is available to those who have successfully completed the courses. This means that the program can count toward your high school diploma or a future college degree just like a regular course. Obviously, this can be very useful, but it's important to note that rules about accepting such credit vary from school to school. Before you commit to a program offering high school credit, check with your guidance counselor to see if your school will accept it. As for programs offering college credit, check with your chosen college (if you have one) to see if they will accept it.

Eligibility and Qualifications

The main eligibility requirement to be concerned about is age or grade in school. A term frequently used in relation to grade level is "rising," as in "rising senior" (someone who will be a senior when the next school year begins). This is especially important where summer programs are concerned. A number of university-based programs make admissions decisions partly in consideration of GPA, class rank, and standardized test scores. This is mentioned in the listings, but you must contact the program for specific numbers. If you are worried that your GPA or your ACT scores, for example, aren't good enough, don't let them stop you from applying to programs that consider such things in the admissions process. Often, a fine essay or even an example of your dedication and eagerness can compensate for statistical weaknesses.

Facilities

We tell you where you'll be living, studying, eating, and having fun during these programs, but there isn't enough room to go into all the details. Some of those details can be important: what is and isn't accessible for people with disabilities, whether the site of a summer program has air-conditioning, and how modern the laboratory and computer equipment are. You can expect most program brochures and application materials to address these concerns, but if you still have questions about the facilities, just call the program's administration and ask.

Financial Details

While a few of the programs listed here are fully underwritten by collegiate and corporate sponsors, most of them rely on you for at least some of their funding.

Prices and fees for 2005 are listed here, but bear in mind that costs rise slightly almost every year. You and your parents must take costs into consideration when choosing a program. We always try to note where financial aid is available, but really, most programs do their best to ensure that a shortage of funds does not prevent qualified applicants from taking part.

Residential versus Commuter Options

Simply put, some programs prefer that participating students live with other participants and staff members, others do not, and still others leave the decision entirely to the students themselves. As a rule, residential programs are suitable for young people who live out of town or even out of state, as well as for local residents. They generally provide a better overview of college life than programs in which you're only on campus for a few hours a day, and they're a way to test how well you cope with living away from home. Commuter programs may be viable only if you live near the program site or if you can stay with relatives who do. Bear in mind that for residential programs especially, the travel between your home and the location of the activity is almost always your responsibility and can significantly increase the cost of participation.

❏ FINALLY . . .

Ultimately, there are three important things to bear in mind concerning all of the programs listed in this volume. The first is that things change. Staff members come and go, funding is added or withdrawn, supply and demand determine which programs continue and which are terminated. Dates, times, and costs vary for many reasons. Because of this, the information we give you, although as current and detailed as possible, is just not enough on which to base your final decision. If you are interested in a program, you simply must write, call, fax, or e-mail the organization concerned to get the latest and most complete information available. This has the added benefit of putting you in touch with someone who can deal with your individual questions and problems.

Another important point to keep in mind when considering these programs is that the people who run them provided the information printed here. The editors of this book haven't attended the programs and don't endorse them: we simply give you the information with which to begin your own research. And after all, we can't pass judgment because you're the only one who can decide which programs are right for you.

The final thing to bear in mind is that the programs listed here are just the tip of the iceberg. No book can possibly cover all of the opportunities that are available to you—partly because they are so numerous and are constantly coming and going, and partly because some are waiting to be discovered. For instance, you may be very interested in taking a college course but don't see the college that interests you in the listings. Call their Admissions Office! Even if they don't have a special program for high school students, they might be able to make some kind of arrangements for you to visit or sit in on a class. Use the ideas behind these listings and take the initiative to turn them into opportunities!

❑ THE PROGRAMS

American Jail Association (AJA)

Membership

Full-time college students who are not currently employed in the field of corrections are eligible for student membership. Members receive a subscription to *American Jails* magazine.

> **American Jail Association**
> 1135 Professional Court
> Hagerstown, MD 21740-5853
> 301-790-3930
> http://www.corrections.com/aja/
>   index.shtml

American Police Hall of Fame and Museum

Membership

Membership in the Hall of Fame and Museum is open to anyone who has an interest in law enforcement. Membership benefits include free admission to the museum and a quarterly newsletter.

> **American Police Hall of Fame and Museum**
> 6350 Horizon Drive
> Titusville, FL 32780-8002
> 321-264-0911
> policeinfo@aphf.org
> http://www.aphf.org/museum.html

Boston University High School Honors Program

College Courses/Summer Study

Rising high school seniors can participate in the High School Honors Program, which offers six-week, for-credit undergraduate study at the university. Students take two for-credit classes (up to eight credits) alongside regular Boston University students, live in dorms on campus, and participate in extracurricular activities and tours of local attractions. Recent courses included Criminal Law, Victimology, Terrorism, and various foreign languages. The program typically begins in early July. Students who demonstrate financial need may be eligible for financial aid. Tuition for the program is approximately $3,550, plus registration/program fees ($350) and room and board options ($1,598 to $1,718). Visit the university's Summer Programs Web site for more information.

> **Boston University High School Honors Program**
> 755 Commonwealth Avenue
> Boston, MA 02215-1401
> 617-353-5124
> summer@bu.edu
> http://www.bu.edu/summer/
>   highschool

Central Intelligence Agency (CIA) Undergraduate Scholar Program

Employment and Internship Opportunities

If you're interested in working in an intelligence-related career, the Central Intelligence Agency's Undergraduate Scholar Program will help you get an introduction to the world of work and the intelligence community. High school seniors planning to enter a four- or five-year college program, as well as college sophomores, may apply. The program was originally developed for minority and disabled students, but is available now to everyone. Those accepted into the program become part of the U.S. foreign intelligence effort by working for the CIA full time every summer of their undergraduate career. Transportation to and from Washington, D.C., is provided along with a housing allowance. Participants receive a salary, college tuition up to $18,000 annually, and a full-time position with the agency upon graduation from college.

To qualify, you must be a U.S. citizen, 18 years of age by April 1 of your senior year, and in need of financial assistance for college tuition. Furthermore, you must have a GPA of 3.0 or higher (on a 4.0 scale) and SAT scores of at least 1000 or ACT scores of at least 21. While taking part in the program, you must maintain a college GPA of 2.75 or higher and meet the same performance standards as CIA employees in comparable positions.

In order for you to be considered, the CIA must receive your cover letter, résumé, and a copy of your current academic transcript with standardized test scores by November 1. There is no application form. Visit the program's Web site for more information.

CIA Undergraduate Scholar Program
http://www.odci.gov/employment/
jobs/students_scholar.html

Cornell University Summer College for High School Students
College Courses/Summer Study

As part of its Summer College for High School Students, Cornell University offers an Exploration in Law and the Legal Profession for students who have completed their sophomore, junior, or senior years. The Summer College session runs for six weeks from late June until early August. It is largely a residential program designed to acquaint you with all aspects of college life. The "Exploration in Law and the Legal Profession" seminar is one of several such seminars offered by Cornell to allow students to survey various disciplines within the field and to speak with working professionals. The seminar meets several times per week and includes trial exercises and field trips to courtrooms and prisons. In addition, Summer College participants take two college-level courses of their own choosing, one of which should be in psychology, government, sociology, or a related area to complement the law focus. These are regular undergraduate courses condensed into a very short time span, so they are especially challenging and demanding. Cornell University awards letter grades and full undergraduate credit for the two courses you complete. Residents live and eat on campus, and enjoy access to Cornell's recreational facilities and special activities. Academic fees total around $4,785, while housing, food, and recreation fees amount to an additional $2,465. Books, travel, and an application fee are extra. A very limited amount of financial aid is available. Applications are due in early May, although Cornell advises that you submit them well in advance of the deadline; those applying for financial aid must submit their applications by April 1. Further information and details of the application procedure are available from the Summer College office.

Cornell University Summer College for High School Students
Summer College
B20 Day Hall
Ithaca, NY 14853-2801
607-255-6203
http://www.sce.cornell.edu/sc

Exploration Summer Programs (ESP) at Yale University
College Courses/Summer Study
Exploration Summer Programs has been offering academic summer enrichment programs to students for nearly 30 years. Rising high school sophomores, juniors, and seniors can participate in ESP's Senior Program at Yale University. Two three-week residential and day sessions are available and are typically held in June and July. Participants can choose from more than 80 courses in a variety of areas of study. Recent safety- and security-related courses included Crime Scene Investigation–Forensic Science; Spy Games–Cryptography; and May It Please the Court–Mock Trial. Students entering the 11th or 12th grades can take college seminars, which provide course work that is similar to that of first-year college study. All courses and seminars are ungraded and not for credit. In addition to academics, students participate in extracurricular activities such as tours, sports,

concerts, weekend recreational trips, college trips, and discussions of current events and other issues. Tuition for the Residential Senior Program is approximately $4,100 for one session and $7,400 for two sessions. Day-session tuition ranges from approximately $2,100 for one session to $3,795 for two sessions. A limited number of need-based partial and full scholarships are available. Programs are also available for students in grades four through nine. Contact ESP for more information.

Exploration Summer Programs
470 Washington Street, PO Box 368
Norwood, MA 02062-0368
781-762-7400
http://www.explo.org

Federal Bureau of Investigation
The Federal Bureau of Investigation (FBI) offers its ten-week Volunteer Internship Program to highly motivated high school, college, and graduate students. Interns learn about a variety of careers within the FBI while working alongside special agents and other staff. For quailification and application information, visit the Web site below.

FBI Volunteer Internship Program
http://www.fbijobs.gov/239.asp#4

Health Occupations Students of America (HOSA)
Competition, Conference, Membership
HOSA has been working since 1976 "to promote career opportunities in the health care industry and to enhance the delivery of quality health care to all people." It

is an integral part of the health occupations curriculum in its member schools. The organization offers a variety of competitions at the state and national levels. Qualifying HOSA participants compete in skills and leadership training, and related events, including CPR/First Aid, Medical Spelling, Medical Math, Medical Terminology, First Aid/Rescue Breathing, Personal Care, Practical Nursing, Nursing Assisting, Speaking Skills, Job Seeking Skills, and Interviewing Skills. HOSA also sponsors an annual National Conference and also teams with a variety of organizations to offer scholarships. To participate in HOSA events, you must work with your school, so speak to a counselor or teacher about your interest in the organization.

Health Occupations Students of America
6021 Morriss Road, Suite 111
Flower Mound, TX 75028-3764
800-321-HOSA
http://www.hosa.org

Learning for Life Exploring Program
Field Experience
Learning for Life's Exploring Program is a career exploration program that allows young people to work closely with community organizations to learn life skills and explore careers. Opportunities are available in Fire Service Exploring, Law Enforcement Exploring, and Health Career Exploring. Each Program has five areas of emphasis: Career Opportunities, Service Learning, Leadership Experience, Life Skills, and Character Education. As a participant

in one of these programs, you will work closely with safety professionals and learn about the demands and rewards of a career in the field. Activities in which you might participate include assisting in crowd control at a community event, staffing crime prevention exhibits and tours, providing administrative support in record keeping, learning first aid, helping to organize first aid or firefighting equipment, assisting with fire prevention seminars, and participating in a variety of other tasks.

To be eligible to participate in these programs, you must have completed the eighth grade and be 14 years old *or* be 15 years of age but have not reached your 21st birthday. This program is open to both males and females.

To find a Learning for Life office in your area (there are more than 300 located throughout the United States), contact the Learning for Life Exploring Program.

Learning for Life Exploring Program
1325 West Walnut Hill Lane,
   PO Box 152079
Irving, TX 75015-2079
972-580-2433
http://www.learningforlife.org/
   exploring

MEDCAMP
Camps
Arizona high school students in their junior and senior years have the opportunity to attend MEDCAMP during their summer vacation. The University of Arizona Health Sciences Center (AHSC) has sponsored this free, three-day career camp

every July since 1992. High schools around the state nominate one boy and one girl for the program; the nominees may then submit an application and essay, by which the final participants are selected. If you are chosen to attend MEDCAMP, you will then explore medical careers while living on the University of Arizona campus under the supervision of medical students. During the day, there are classes, laboratory experiences, hospital tours, and opportunities to speak with and watch health care professionals at work. You leave with a better overall understanding of the health care industry and information on specific careers such as nursing, physical and occupational therapy, and pharmacy. If you are interested in attending MEDCAMP, talk to your science teacher, who should receive nomination forms from the AHSC.

MEDCAMP
University of Arizona Health
    Sciences Center
Office of Public Affairs
1501 North Campbell Avenue, PO
    Box 245095
Tucson, AZ 85724-5095
520-626-7301
riley@u.arizona.edu
http://www.ahsc.arizona.edu/opa/
    medcamp

National Association of Emergency Medical Technicians (NAEMT)

Membership

The association offers membership to EMT students who can prove enrollment in an EMS program. Members receive access to association publications, an e-mail listserv, and educational opportunities. Contact the association for more information.

**National Association of
    Emergency Medical
    Technicians**
PO Box 1400
Clinton, MS 39060-1400
800-346-2368
info@naemt.org
http://www.naemt.org

SkillsUSA

Competitions

SkillsUSA offers "local, state and national competitions in which students demonstrate occupational and leadership skills." Students who participate in its SkillsUSA Championships can compete in categories such as Basic Health Care Skills, Community Service, Criminal Justice, and First Aid/CPR. (Additionally, Firefighting is also available as a full-participation, demonstration contest.) SkillsUSA works directly with high schools and colleges, so ask your guidance counselor or teacher if it is an option for you. Visit the SkillsUSA Web site for more information.

SkillsUSA
PO Box 3000
Leesburg, VA 20177-0300
703-777-8810
http://www.skillsusa.org

Society of Fire Protection Engineers (SPFE)

Membership

The society provides offers free electronic membership to students of all ages who are interested in fire protection engineering. Members receive access to technical areas of the society's Web site and publications.

Society of Fire Protection Engineers
7315 Wisconsin Avenue, Suite 620E
Bethesda, MD 20814-3234
301-718-2910
sfpehqtrs@sfpe.org
http://www.sfpe.org

Summer College for High School Students at Syracuse University

College Courses/Summer Study

The Syracuse University Summer College for High School Students features a Forensics Science Program for those who have just completed their sophomore, junior, or senior year. The Summer College runs for six weeks and offers a residential option so participants can experience campus life while still in high school. The Forensics Science Program has several aims: to introduce you to the science behind criminal investigation; to help you match your aptitudes with possible careers; and to prepare you for college, both academically and socially. You will participate in classes, attend lectures, complete laboratory exercises, and gather evidence as a member of a crime scene team at a simulated crime scene. Topics of study include blood analysis, organic and inorganic evidence analysis, microscopic investigations, hair analysis, DNA, drug chemistry and toxicology, fiber comparisons, paints, glass compositions and fragmentation, fingerprints, soil

comparisons, and arson investigations. College credit is awarded for completion of the program. Admission is competitive and is based on recommendations, test scores, and transcripts. The total cost of the residential program is about $5,300; the commuter option costs about $3,800. Some scholarships are available. The application deadline is in mid-May, or mid-April for those seeking financial aid. For further information, contact the Summer College.

Summer College for High School Students at Syracuse University
111 Waverly Avenue, Suite 240
Syracuse, NY 13244-2320
315-443-5297
sumcoll@syr.edu
http://summercollege.syr.edu/
    forensic.html

Summer Study at Pennsylvania State University

College Courses/Summer Study

High school students who are interested in careers in criminal justice and other fields can apply to participate in Penn State's Summer Study programs. The six-and-a-half-week College Credit Program begins in late June and recently offered the following public safety–related classes: Intro to the American Criminal Justice System; Human Body: Form And Function; Psychology; Criminology; and Spanish. Students typically choose one course for college credit (for three or four credits) and either an enrichment class/workshop or the Kaplan SAT prep class.

Students who have completed the 10th, 11th, and 12th grades are eligible to apply. The three-and-a-half-week Non-Credit Enrichment Program is held in early July and features public safety–related classes such as Community Service Workshop, Health & Wellness, and Law & The Justice System. Students who have completed the 9th, 10th, and 11th grades are eligible for the program. Tuition for the College Credit Program is approximately $6,000, while tuition for the Non-Credit Enrichment Program is approximately $4,000. Limited financial aid is available. Contact the program for more information.

Summer Study Program
Pennsylvania State University
University Park, PA 16804
800-666-2556
info@summerstudy.com
http://www.summerstudy.com/
   pennstate

U.S. Department of State's Cooperative Education Program
Employment and Internship Opportunities

The Cooperative Education Program integrates and coordinates academic studies with on-the-job experience. To participate in this program, you must be a U.S. citizen, be enrolled in your school's cooperative education program, be in good academic standing, and pass a background check. Cooperative opportunities are available to high school through graduate students. This program offers great employment flexibility, with full- and part-time work options available.

Contact your school's co-op coordinator (probably your guidance counselor) or the U.S. Department of State's cooperative program coordinator for more information; you can also sign up at the department's Web site to receive e-mail updates regarding the Program.

U.S. Department of State
Attn: Cooperative Program
   Coordinator
Recruitment Division, SA-1
2401 E Street NW, Suite 518H
Washington, DC 20522-0001
http://www.careers.state.gov/
   student/programs/coop_edu.html

U.S. Department of State's Stay-in-School Program
Employment and Internship Opportunities

The Stay-in-School Program is designed for students who require financial assistance to continue their education. (Note: Students with a disability do not need to demonstrate financial need to participate in this program.) In this program, you may work in technical, clerical, or administrative positions part time during the school year or full time during the holidays and summer vacation. To be eligible for this program, you must be a U.S. citizen, pass a background check, and be enrolled in a high school, vocational school, or undergraduate program. Contact your guidance counselor or state employment service to learn more about the financial criteria. Contact the Stay-in-School Program coordinator for more information; you can also sign up at the department's Web site to receive e-mail updates regarding the program.

U.S. Department of State
Attn: Stay-in-School Program
    Coordinator
Recruitment Division, SA-1
2401 E Street NW, Suite 518H
Washington, DC 20522-0001
http://www.careers.state.gov/student/
    programs/stay_in_school.html

U.S. Department of State's Summer Clerical Program

Employment and Internship Opportunities

The Summer Clerical Program allows young people to work in office support positions in which they gain work experience and a better understanding of how the State Department works. Participants work during the summer and over the holidays. Typical duties might include the following: answering telephones and performing other receptionist-related duties; filing and maintaining office files; typing and/or using a computer terminal to perform office functions; reviewing outgoing correspondence for correct format, grammar, punctuation, and typographical errors; and photocopying and assembling reports and briefings. To be eligible for this program, you must be a U.S. citizen, be 16 years of age or older at the time of appointment, be enrolled in or accepted at a postsecondary program, and pass a background check. Applications are due by February 1 in the year in which you wish to begin work. Contact the Summer Clerical Program coordinator for more information; you can also sign up at the department's Web site to receive e-mail updates regarding the program.

U.S. Department of State
Attn: Summer Clerical Program
    Coordinator
Recruitment Division, SA-1
2401 E Street NW, Suite 518 H
Washington, DC 20522-0001
http://www.careers.state.gov/student/
    programs/summer_clerical.html

Read a Book

When it comes to finding out about security and safety careers, don't overlook a book. (You're reading one now, after all.) What follows is a short, annotated list of books and periodicals related to public safety. The books range from fiction to personal accounts of what it's like to be a firefighter or FBI agent, to professional volumes on specific topics, such as crime analysis techniques and studying for exams. Don't be afraid to check out the professional journals, either. The technical stuff may be way above your head right now, but if you take the time to become familiar with one or two, you're bound to pick up some of what is important to safety personnel and to begin to feel like a part of their world, which is what you're interested in, right?

We've tried to include recent materials as well as old favorites. Always check for the most recent editions, and, if you find an author you like, ask your librarian to help you find more. Keep reading good books!

❑ BOOKS

Ackerman, Thomas H. *FBI Careers: The Ultimate Guide to Landing a Job as One of America's Finest.* 2d ed. Indianapolis, Ind.: JIST Works, 2005. This book provides information on careers in the Federal Bureau of Investigation.

Adams, Sam. *War of Numbers: An Intelligence Memoir.* South Royalton, Vt.: Steerforth Press, 1998. A fascinating account about a CIA controversy in Vietnam that takes stock of how intelligence may be collected, collated, interpreted, and sometimes ignored.

Baker, Thomas E. *Introductory Criminal Analysis: Crime Prevention and Intervention Strategies.* Upper Saddle River, N.J.: Prentice Hall, 2004. Provides an overview of criminal analysis.

Barkan, Steven E. *Criminology: A Sociological Understanding.* 3d ed. Upper Saddle River, N.J.: Prentice Hall, 2005. An up-to-date textbook that treats social structure and social inequalities as central themes in the study of crime. An essential introduction to crime analysis.

Bishop, Matt. *Introduction to Computer Security.* Upper Saddle River, N.J.: Addison-Wesley Professional, 2004. An introduction to the art and science of information security—a critical area of focus for law enforcement officials in the age of terrorism and cybercrime.

Boba, Rachel. *Crime Analysis and Crime Mapping.* Thousand Oaks, Calif.: Sage, 2005. This book provides an overview of crime analysis and crime mapping for undergraduate and graduate students taking courses in criminology, criminal justice, forensic science, criminal investigation, geographic information systems, geography, and sociology.

Britz, Marjie T. *Computer Forensics and Cyber Crime: An Introduction.* Upper Saddle River, N.J.: Prentice Hall, 2003. A thorough examination of computer-related crime.

Brown, Larry. *On Fire.* New York: Warner Books, 1995. In this complex and moving memoir, Brown recounts his 17 years as a fireman in Oxford, Mississippi.

Camenson, Blythe. *Firefighting.* VGM Career Portraits. New York: McGraw-Hill, 1999. Presents information on the various duties of firefighters, including emergency medical services, fire investigation and prevention, training, and administration.

Combs, Cindy C. *Terrorism in the 21st Century.* 3d ed. Prentice Hall, 2002. Provides an unbiased examination of contemporary terrorism.

Cornelius, Gary F. *Stressed Out: Strategies for Living and Working in Corrections.* 2d ed. Lanham, Md.: American Correctional Association, 2005. Provides practical advice to corrections officers and managers on how to reduce stress in the workplace.

Corrections Officer Exam. New York: Learning Express, 2004. A useful study guide to the exam that also offers insight into what a corrections officer can expect after passing it.

Cromwell, Paul, ed. *In Their Own Words: Criminals On Crime.* 4th ed. Los Angeles: Roxbury, 2005. This anthology provides an inside look at the criminal mind.

DeHaan, John D. *Kirk's Fire Investigation.* 5th ed. Upper Saddle River, N.J.: Prentice Hall, 2002. Widely considered to be the definitive textbook on fire investigation.

Delattre, Edwin J. *Character and Cops: Ethics in Policing.* 4th ed. Washington, D.C.: American Enterprise Institute Press, 2002. An interesting overview of ethical issues in law enforcement and police training in the United States.

Douglas, John. *John Douglas's Guide to Landing a Career in Law Enforcement.* New York: McGraw-Hill, 2004. A renowned FBI profiler provides advice to those interested in pursuing careers in law enforcement. Includes an overview of law enforcement agencies and careers; worksheets, checklists, and self-evaluations; and useful Web sites and other resources.

Ertel, Mike, and Gregory C. Berk. *Firefighting: Basic Skills and Techniques.* Tinley Park, Ill.: Goodheart-Willcox, 1998. A useful survey of the field, providing the basic guidelines of fire extinction and safety.

Ferrell, Jeff, and Clinton Sanders, et. al. (eds.). *Cultural Criminology Unleashed.* London: GlassHouse Press, 2005. A worthwhile text in the study of crime that collects important essays on how crime relates to various cultural forms—particularly the media.

Geeting, James. *The Badge: Thoughts from a State Trooper.* Indian Wells, Calif.: McKenna, 2003. A Wyoming State Trooper discusses the rewards and challenges of his career.

Hammett, Dashiell. *Dashiell Hammett: Crime Stories and Other Writings.* New York: Library of America, 2001. Sharp, detailed, and gripping stories—by a master storyteller—about criminals and cops.

Harr, J. Scott, and Karen M. Hess. *Careers In Criminal Justice And Related Fields: From Internship to Promotion.* 5th ed. Belmont, Calif.: Wadsworth, 2005. Provides practical advice to students interested in pursuing careers in criminal justice.

Hutton, Donald B., and Anna Mydlarz. *Guide to Homeland Security Careers.* Hauppauge, N.Y.: Barrons Educational Series, 2003. This book details career opportunities in homeland security.

International Foundation of Protection Officers. *Protection Officer Training Manual.* 7th ed. Oxford, U.K.: Butterworth-Heinemann, 2003. A useful and thorough guide to private security service careers and preventive police work.

Ivey, Pat. *EMT: Rescue.* New York: eReads.com, 2002. Offers true minute-by-minute accounts of mobile rescues.

Jeffreys, Diarmuid. *The Bureau: Inside the Modern FBI.* Charlotte, N.C.: Replica Books, 2001. Takes readers on a whirlwind tour of the modern FBI. Full of fascinating anecdotes and information.

Kerins, Devin. *EMS: The Job of Your Life.* Poughkeepsie, N.Y.: Vivisphere, 2002. This book provides a behind-the-scenes look at the world of emergency medical services.

Kerle, Ken. *Exploring Jail Operations.* Hagerstown, Md.: American Jail Association, 2003. Provides an overview of jail operations for students and jail practitioners. Topics discussed include jail history, jail systems, women in jail work, inspections, technology, cultural diversity, and legal issues.

Kessler, Ronald. *The Bureau: The Secret History of the FBI.* New York: St. Martin's Paperbacks, 2003. A comprehensive examination and history of the Federal Bureau of Investigation.

Krauss, Erich. *On the Line: Inside the U.S. Border Patrol.* New York: Citadel Press, 2004. An insightful and informative overview of the profession, including a detailed history of immigration in the United States.

Lindsay, Paul. *Code Name: Gentkill: A Novel of the FBI.* New York: Villard, 1995. A gripping novel about a serial murderer who is systematically gunning down FBI agents, and the agent who must stop him.

Maclean, Norman. *Young Men and Fire.* Chicago: University Of Chicago Press, 1992. A captivating nonfiction account of the Mann Gulch, Montana, fire that claimed the lives of 13 young smoke-jumpers on August 5, 1949.

Maynard, Gary D. *Correction Officer.* 14th ed. New York: Arco , 2002. The first choice of correction officers for more than 40 years, this thorough book is filled with valuable and current information about test-taking practices. Includes sample exams, detailed explanations, and illustrations.

Melanson, Philip H., and Peter F. Stevens. *The Secret Service: The Hidden History of an Enigmatic Agency.* New

York: Carroll & Graf, 2003. A history of the Secret Service from its creation in 1865 to today.

Osborne, Deborah, and Susan Wernicke. *Introduction to Crime Analysis: Basic Resources for Criminal Justice Practice.* Binghamton, N.Y.: Haworth Press, 2003. A practical resource guide for new crime analysts.

Peat, Barbara. *From College to Career: A Guide For Criminal Justice Majors.* Boston: Allyn and Bacon, 2004. Provides career information, résumé-building exercises, interactive worksheets, and assignments.

Petro, Joseph, and Jeffrey Robinson. *Standing Next To History: An Agent's Life Inside the Secret Service.* New York: Thomas Dunne Books, 2005. An engaging memoir detailing an agent's 23 years in the Secret Service.

Pistone, Joseph D., with Richard Woodley. *Donnie Brasco: My Undercover Life in the Mafia.* New York: Signet Books, 1997. The book on which the well-known movie was based. An unforgettable account of how an undercover FBI agent became a part of the mysterious, deadly world of the mafia he was trained to expose.

Schroeder, Donald J., and Frank A. Lombardo. *How to Prepare for the Police Officer Examination.* 6th ed. Hauppauge, N.Y.: Barron's Educational Series, 2001. Essential reading for anyone who aspires to a police career; presents general information, strategies for achieving a high score on competitive police exams, and four full-length exams.

Smith, Dennis. *Firefighters: Their Lives in Their Own Words.* New York: Broadway Books, 2002. A wide-ranging collection of interviews that offers an emotional portrait of these uniquely dedicated public servants.

Snow, Robert L. *SWAT Teams: Explosive Face-Offs With America's Deadliest Criminals.* New York: Perseus Books Group, 2000. This book provides an inside look at our nation's SWAT teams.

Stephens, W. Richard, Jr. *Careers in Criminal Justice.* Boston: Allyn and Bacon, 2002. Provides detailed information on a wide variety of careers in criminal justice.

Stering, Robert S. *Police Officer's Handbook: An Introductory Guide.* Sudbury, Mass.: Jones and Bartlett, 2004. This book provides readers with an introduction to the world of police work.

Stinchcomb, Jeanne. *Corrections: Past, Present and Future.* Lanham, Md.: American Correctional Association, 2005. A comprehensive overview of the correctional system for students.

Titus Reid, Sue. *Crime and Criminology.* 11th ed. New York: McGraw-Hill, 2005. Accessible and engaging textbook covering traditional areas of criminology as well as questions of popular concern and contemporary police debate.

White, Jonathan R. *Terrorism: An Introduction.* Belmont, Calif.: Wadsworth, 2002. Provides a detailed introduction to terrorism and countermeasures by law enforcement professionals.

❏ PERIODICALS

American Jails Magazine. Published bimonthly by the American Jail Association, 1135 Professional Court, Hagerstown, MD 21740-5853, 301-790-3930, http://www.corrections.com/aja/publications/magazine.shtml. This publication covers day-to-day management and operations of detention facilities in the United States and the world.

Arrest Law Bulletin. Published monthly by the Quinlan Publishing Group, 23 Drydock Avenue, Boston, MA 02210-2387, info@quinlan.com, http://www.quinlan.com. Sheds light on what does and does not constitute a lawful arrest, by examining court cases that cover such issues as probable cause, warrantless arrests, and investigative stops.

Corrections Compendium. Published six times annually by the American Correctional Association, 4380 Forbes Boulevard, Lanham, MD 20706-4322, 301-918-1800, http://www.aca.org/publications/ccjournal.asp. This publication features articles, book reviews, commentary, corrections news, and profiles of corrections and criminal justice agencies throughout the world.

Corrections Today. Published seven times annually by the American Correctional Association, 4380 Forbes Boulevard, Lanham, MD 20706-4322, 301-918-1800, http://www.aca.org/publications/ctmagazine.asp. This publication provides news and updates regarding the world of corrections.

Criminal Victimization. Published annually by the Bureau of Justice Statistics, U.S. Department of Justice, http://www.ojp.usdoj.gov/bjs/cvict-gen.htm. An indispensable statistical report summarizing criminal victimization rates and levels, including findings about the characteristics of victims.

The Criminologist. Published six times annually by the American Society of Criminology, 1314 Kinnear Road, Columbus, OH 43212-1156, http://www.asc41.com/publications.html. This publication for members details societal activities and developments in the profession.

Criminology: An Interdisciplinary Journal. Published quarterly by the American Society of Criminology, 1314 Kinnear Road, Columbus, OH 43212-1156, http://www.asc41.com/publications.html. This publication focuses on crime and deviant behavior (as found in sociology, psychology, design, systems analysis) and decision theory (as applied to crime and criminal justice).

FireRescue Magazine. Published monthly by Jems Communications, 525 B Street, Suite 1900, San Diego, CA 92101, 888-456-5367, http://www.jems.com. This magazine provides a variety of resources to firefighters, including how-to features, monthly apparatus profiles, hands-on firefighting articles, and rescue reports/profiles.

Fire Technology. Published quarterly by Springer Science+Business Media B.V. (journals-ny@springer-sbm.com, http://www.springerlink.com) for the National Fire Protection Association.

This peer-reviewed publication examines fire science from the perspectives of physics, chemistry, engineering, and ergonomics.

The Forecaster. Published quarterly by the International Association of Crime Analysts, 9218 Metcalf Avenue, #364, Overland Park, KS 66212-1476, 800-609-3419, http://www.iaca.net. This publication provides information and updates on crime analysis to association members.

Governing. Published monthly by Congressional Quarterly, Inc., 1100 Connecticut Avenue NW, #1300, Washington, DC 20036-4109, 888-955-4688, customerservice@governing.com, http://www.governing.com. A leading information source for state and local government that explains the inner machinations of law enforcement: how it works, what it costs, and why.

Homeland First Response. Published bimonthly by Jems Communications, 525 B Street, Suite 1900, San Diego, CA 92101-4495, 888-456-5367, http://www.jems.com/Columnists/homelandfirstresponse. This publication provides useful articles for homeland security professionals.

International Fire Fighter. Published four times annually by MDM Publishing Ltd. (http://www.iffmag.com) for the International Association of Firefighters. This publication provides a comprehensive overview of fire fighting throughout the world.

Jems: Journal of Emergency Medicine. Published monthly by Jems Communications, 525 B Street, Suite 1900, San Diego, CA 92101-4495, 888-456-5367, http://www.jems.com. A terrific journal for anyone interested in emergency medical services (EMS) careers, offering firsthand accounts from the field, special features about the daily lives of EMS workers, and articles about vehicles and equipment, medical developments, and innovations in emergency care.

Law Enforcement Bulletin. Published monthly by the Federal Bureau of Investigation, 935 Pennsylvania Avenue NW, Washington, DC, 20035-0001, http://www.fbi.gov/publications/leb/leb.htm. Produced and written by the agency, this publication offers opinions, firsthand accounts from the field, special articles about developments in FBI training and practice, and job opportunities within various divisions.

Law Officer. Published bimonthly by Jems Communications, 525 B Street, Suite 1900, San Diego, CA 92101-4495, 888-456-5367, http://www.jems.com. This magazine provides articles on the best in tactics, technology, and training for law officers.

NAEMT News. Published six times annually by the National Association of Emergency Medical Technicians, PO Box 1400, Clinton, MS 39060-1400. Provides coverage of developments in emergency medical care and association activities for members. Visit http://www.naemt.org/publications to read a sample issue.

Narcotics Law Bulletin. Published monthly by the Quinlan Publishing Group, 23 Drydock Avenue, Boston,

MA 02210-2387, info@quinlan.com, http://www.quinlan.com/b_nlb.html. This publication covers such topics as drug arrests and prosecutions, air surveillance and other investigative tactics, and more.

National Fire Protection Association Journal. Published bimonthly by the National Fire Protection Association, 1 Batterymarch Park, Quincy, MA 02169-7471, 800-344-3555, http://www.nfpa.org. Examines issues and developments in fire protection engineering.

The Police Chief. Published monthly by the International Association of Chiefs of Police, 515 North Washington Street, Alexandria, VA 22314, 703-836-6767. Features news, columns, book reviews, and commentary for police chiefs on law enforcement-related issues. Visit http://www.policechiefmagazine.org to read sample articles.

Police Department Disciplinary Bulletin. Published monthly by the Quinlan Publishing Group, 23 Drydock Avenue, Boston, MA 02210-2387, info@quinlan.com, http://www.quinlan.com/b_pddb.html. Discusses the when and how of disciplining officers, avoid-

ing disciplinary problems, and related subjects.

Sheriff. Published bimonthly by the National Sheriff's Association, 1450 Duke Street, Alexandria, VA 22314-3490, 703-836-7827, http://www.sheriffs.org/pub-magazine.shtml. Covers issues of interest to law enforcement and criminal justice professionals, including successful law enforcement programs, professional news, and legislative updates.

Wildland Firefighter. Published bimonthly by Jems Communications, 525 B Street, Suite 1900, San Diego, CA 92101-4495, 619-699-6578, wildlandsubscriptions@elsevier.com, http://www.jems.com. Provides an overview of firefighting tactics and strategies as they relate to fighting wildland fires.

Women Police. Published quarterly by the International Association of Women Police, North Deer Isle Road, PO Box 690418, Tulsa, OK 74169-0418, http://www.iawp.org. A journal produced by a fast-growing, dynamic organization that addresses the concerns of women in various areas of police or law enforcement work.

Surf the Web

You must use the Internet to do research, to find things out, to explore. The Internet is the closest you'll get to what's happening right now all around the world. This chapter gets you started with an annotated list of Web sites related to safety and security. Try a few. Follow the links. Maybe even venture as far as asking questions in a chat room. The more you read about and interact with public safety personnel, the better prepared you'll be when you're old enough to participate as a professional.

One caveat: you probably already know that URLs change all the time. If a Web address listed below is out of date, try searching the site's name or other keywords. Chances are, if an address is still out there, you'll find it. If it's not, maybe you'll find something better!

American Police Hall of Fame and Museum
http://www.aphf.org

The American Police Hall of Fame and Museum in Miami, Florida, was created by the American Federation of Police and Concerned Citizens and the National Association of Chiefs of Police. Visit its Web site for a virtual tour of its facilities, a history of policing, interesting statistics, and advice on public safety issues such as travel, guns, crime prevention, and terrorism.

American Red Cross
http://www.redcross.org

The Red Cross is mentioned in the Do It Yourself section for its CPR and first aid courses and the training it provides to young people who want to educate others about various health and safety issues. Its Web site offers a helpful little feature that allows you to type in your zip code and get contact information for the Red Cross office nearest you, so you can get involved right away. This site, which is both extensive and easy to use, also gives you an interesting history lesson via its Red Cross Museum, and puts you in touch with other humanitarian organizations that share this organization's commitment to helping others. The American Red Cross has been an integral part of the country's health and safety efforts since 1881—it has a lot to offer as you explore the field of public safety, and its Web site deserves a look.

Bureau of Alcohol, Tobacco, Firearms and Explosives
http://www.atf.gov/kids/faq.htm

The Bureau of Alcohol, Tobacco, Firearms and Explosives (ATF) has an extremely informative site for kids (and teenagers). You can learn about the history of the ATF, the famous crime fighter

Eliot Ness, and ATF outreach programs, such as the Gang Resistance Education and Training (GREAT) Program. Thousands of law enforcement officers, including many in the ATF, have been trained to present this gang prevention curriculum in classrooms. There's also a description here of how the Department of Justice (ATF's boss) helped establish the Academy of Law, Justice, and Security in 1991, a school-within-a-school at Anacostia High School in Washington, D.C. This is one of about 150 career academies that try to prevent students from joining gangs by offering some of the same things youth seek from gangs: a sense of belonging, peer support, a perceived future, and a way to make a living.

The Central Intelligence Agency (CIA)
http://www.odci.gov

There's something for almost everybody at the CIA Web site. There are answers to FAQs about the agency and intelligence gathering; a CIA Museum, where you can view tools of the spy trade such as matchbox cameras, dead drop spikes, and seismic intruder detection devices; and a virtual tour of the agency's headquarters, where you can see the CIA library, various memorials and statues, and exterior areas of CIA facilities. The Careers section provides an overview of internships, co-op opportunities, and scholarships for college undergraduates. And you can browse through the amazing variety of positions within the CIA, such as language instructor, operational psychologist, collection management officer, counterterror-

ism analyst, paralegal, and geographer. Another useful area is the Library/Reference section, where you can browse online versions of the *World Factbook,* the *Factbook on Intelligence*, and a suggested reading list of intelligence-related literature.

Cool Works®
http://www.coolworks.com

You've probably had a time of it trying to find a summer job that's fun and relevant to your future career of public safety. Cool Works® quickly links you up to a mass of information about seasonal security jobs at dozens of national and state parks, preserves, monuments, and wilderness areas. There are also listings of jobs and volunteer opportunities at ski areas, private resorts, cruise ships, and summer camps. Most of the national and state jobs require that applicants be 18 years or older. Most national and state parks listed here have seasonal positions available in similar departments. Specific job descriptions can also be accessed by searching a pull-down menu of U.S. states and regions or international locations. While only some jobs allow you to apply directly online, many have downloadable application forms.

Corrections.com
http://www.corrections.com

Corrections.com is the largest online resource for corrections. You'll find everything from corrections associations and industry publications to chat rooms and research libraries to legislative updates. There's a very useful Student section where you can submit questions about any topic about corrections or finding an internship, and someone working in the field will answer it. Many of the questions posted are from college students writing research papers or seeking summer jobs. This site might open your eyes to the variety of people working in prisons. For instance, there's actually a whole section devoted to food services and another to correctional technology.

Federal Bureau of Investigation (FBI)
http://www.fbi.gov

Those considering a career as a special agent will learn plenty by combing the pages of this Web site. The Learn About Us section provides background information about the FBI's mission and structure; employment-related information on jobs and necessary qualifications; and specific areas of investigation within the FBI, such as counterterrorism, organized crime, and foreign counterintelligence. You'll also want to look at the list of the FBI's 56 field offices (where most of the hiring occurs) to find out more about the location closest to you. Another section is devoted to the FBI Academy, with information on new agent training. Read it to decide if you're up to the rigors of the 15-week training, which includes academics, firearms training, physical training/defensive tactics, and practical exercises. A special subsite (http://www.fbi.gov/fbikids.htm) for kids (and teenagers) allows you to learn about famous cases (such as the U.S. Embassy Bombing in Kenya in 1998), follow a case from start to finish, learn about FBI history, and watch videos detailing a day in the life of an FBI agent.

FireFighting.com
http://www.firefighting.com

This is a useful site for firefighters and emergency medical workers, with many useful sections and subsections. Feel free to explore the whole site or just take a look at a few of the highlights, like the photo archives of fires, car accidents, and more. You'll want to read the Forum section, an online meeting place for aspiring and current firefighters. The Life Support section helps firefighters reduce stress with useful articles and poems written by firefighters and other emergency professionals.

How Stuff Works
http://people.howstuffworks.com

This site should also be on your short list of Web sites to explore, as it covers how "stuff," as varied and timely as tsunamis to identity theft, works. Complex concepts are carefully broken down and examined, including photos and links to current and past news items about the subject. Subsections of this site detail the inner workings of emergency rooms, burglar alarms, police dogs, riot control, red-light cameras, breathalyzers, facial recognition systems, hostage negotiations, the Mafia, and countless other topics. Best yet, the articles are written by professionals in the field, so you're guaranteed an expert look at the world of public safety.

My Future
http://www.myfuture.com

You want to work in safety and security, but perhaps college just isn't in the cards for you. This colorful site aims to help new high school graduates "jumpstart their lives" with information about alternatives to four-year colleges, such as military opportunities and technical or vocational colleges. In the hefty military career database, you'll find dozens of job descriptions for positions such as emergency management officers, firefighters, emergency management specialists, and law enforcement security officers and specialists. While the site is divided into four main sections—Military Opportunities, Money Matters, Beyond High School, and Career Toolbox—most of the useful stuff is in the career section. For instance, in this section, you can learn about the hottest jobs, strong cover letters, and interview techniques. You can take a career interest quiz to find out if you have a realistic, investigative, artistic, social, enterprising, or conventional work personality. You'll also find some good info in the Money section. In the Money subsection, Living On Your Own, you can learn how to set a budget and live within your means. Or visit the money subsection called Searching for Dollars to get a handle on the financial aid process.

The 9-1-1 Fire Police Medical Web
http://www.the911site.com

Although you can navigate through this site pretty quickly and easily, you should plan on spending a lot of time here: there is just too much information and too many good links to see on a quick visit. As

its name advertises, the 9-1-1 Fire Police Medical Web site covers work in firefighting, law enforcement, and emergency medical services. It also features coverage of severe weather events and other disasters as they occur—very sensible, considering that they require the response of all the emergency services and several other public safety organizations besides. The 9-1-1 Fire Police Medical Web site offers some articles and features of its own, but its outstanding characteristic is its links to other sites, including fire departments in the United States and Canada, general emergency services, sheriff's departments, and EMS 911 dispatchers. There are also links to firefighting brigades around the world and to various online public safety newsletters. It's hard to imagine any emergency services information you couldn't find via this Web site.

Officer.com
http://www.officer.com

You won't find a more valuable, inclusive home page for law enforcement information. This well-organized site is broken into 13 jam-packed subdirectories, such as Agencies, Associations, Criminal Justice, and Special Ops. One subdirectory that might be of particular use to you is Personal Pages, a listing of law officers' home pages, where an astonishing number of officers have posted information about themselves, their jobs, and their departments. Many of these people are willing to be contacted about career opportunities. You can easily search this section since the names are organized alphabetically by state. This would be a great place to find a local police officer who's willing to tell you more about the field.

Peterson's Education Portal
http://www.petersons.com

This site offers anything you want to know about surviving high school, getting into college, and choosing a graduate degree. For information about safety and security in particular, check out the College and Graduate School sections, which offer school directories searchable by keyword, degree, location, tuition, size, GPA, and even sports offered. While this site is not devoted solely to safety and security education, it's worth a visit for its comprehensiveness; school listings offer the usual basics plus details on financial aid, school facilities, student government, faculty, and admissions requirements.

The Princeton Review
http://www.princetonreview.com/
home.asp

This site is everything you want in a high school guidance counselor—it's friendly, well informed, and available to you night and day. Originally a standardized test preparation company, The Princeton Review is now online, giving you frank advice on colleges, careers, and, of course, SATs. Students who've spent their summers and after-school hours volunteering at a clinic or hospital will find good tips here on how to present those extracurricular activities on college application forms. If you're looking for contact with other students who are weighing their options, too, link to one of the discussion

groups on college admissions and careers. Three of The Princeton Review's coolest tools are the Career Quiz, which creates a list of possible careers based on your interests and work style; the Counselor-O-Matic, which reviews your grades, test scores, and extracurricular record to calculate your chances of admission at many colleges; and the Majors Search, which allows you to get an overview of majors such as criminal science and criminology and to locate schools that offer degrees in these and related fields. Also helpful is the list of schools offering online programs and degrees. Get a heads up on the competition by checking out the site's summer program section, specifically geared towards high school students, which lists summer internships, camps, and enrichment programs.

U.S. Border Patrol: A Career with Borders, But No Boundaries
http://honorfirst.com/usbp1.htm

This site offers a comprehensive overview of the U.S. Border Patrol's mission, organization, and history. If working for the Border Patrol is your goal, you'll appreciate the step-by-step outline of the hiring process and the description of new agent training. The Border Patrol's mission is to detect and prevent smuggling and illegal entry of aliens into the United States and to protect our borders from terrorism. This Web site doesn't glamorize the job. It cautions that "border patrol is police work and police work can be dangerous" and that "violence is becoming more of a problem along the border." This site is engaging and clearly intended for someone like you who is exploring the career. It'll even teach you some new terminology like "coyote," a smuggler of illegal aliens.

U.S. Department of Agriculture Forest Service
http://www.fs.fed.us

Did you realize that the Forest Service employs more than 600 people to police federal lands and conduct criminal investigations? Scratch beneath the surface of this mostly text-based government site, and you'll find a useful resource about working as a law enforcement officer for the Forest Service. One area in particular, Employment, is jammed with relevant information on job possibilities, law enforcement, and investigation, as well as a day-in-the-life profile of a special agent. You'll also find information on volunteer opportunities and student employment, as well as other useful resources.

U.S. Department of Homeland Security
http://www.dhs.gov/dhspublic/index.jsp

The Department of Homeland Security was created to help protect Americans from terrorist threats, as well as to provide assistance during and after natural disasters and terrorist attacks. Visit its Web site to read about the wide variety of issues facing workers in this key government agency and the career options available at the many agencies that fall under its jurisdiction, including U.S. Customs and Border Protection, U.S. Immigration and Customs Enforcement, the U.S. Transportation Security Administration, the Federal Emergency Management Agency, the U.S. Coast Guard, and the U.S. Secret Service.

U.S. Marshals for Students of All Ages
http://www.usmarshals.gov/usmsforkids/index.html

The United States Marshals Service is the oldest (1789) federal law enforcement agency in the United States. At its student Web site, you can read a history of the U.S. Marshals, learn more about their job duties (which include fugitive investigations, judicial security, witness security, prisoner services, asset forfeiture, and special operations support), and get inside information on how to land a job in the Marshals Service.

U.S. News & World Report: America's Best Colleges
http://www.usnews.com/usnews/edu/college/majors/majors_index_brief.php

Use this free online service to search schools by national ranking, location, name, or major. (The link above will allow you to search by major.) The Security and Protective Services subsection alone lists more than 500 schools that offer safety- and security-related programs, and each school link includes contact information and details about services and facilities, campus life, mission, and extracurricular activities. Note: In order to read the full account information about each school, you must either buy the print publication or pay for the Premium Online Edition.

U.S. Secret Service
http://www.secretservice.gov

Secret Service agents not only protect our elected officials, but they also participate in criminal investigations involving law enforcement, administration, intelligence, forensics, security, information technology, communications, and other specialized areas. Visit the Secret Service's Web site for a history of the profession, a detailed overview of careers in the Secret Service, and answers to frequently asked questions, such as What is it like to be a Secret Service agent? What do I have to do to become a Secret Service agent? What kind of training do agents get? and Do you have to be good at math to be an agent? The Web site also has interesting sections on counterfeiting, forensics, financial crimes, and cyber terrorism. This is a useful Web site that provides information on an often misunderstood federal agency.

Yahoo!: Government: Intelligence
http://dir.yahoo.com/Government/
    Intelligence

It might seem odd to include the popular search engine Yahoo! among a list of safety and security Web sites, but you'll change your mind after you've visited it. If you're hungry for more after reading this chapter and visiting the sites listed here, surf on over to Yahoo!

Yahoo! has done a tremendous amount of legwork for you. For example, if you're interested in information warfare and cyberterrorism, you can surf to one of the more than 15 sites currently included here. You'll also find links to government intelligence organizations, museums, and journals and magazines.

Ask for Money

By the time most students get around to thinking about applying for scholarships, they have already extolled their personal and academic virtues to such lengths in essays and interviews for college applications that even their own grandmothers wouldn't recognize them. The thought of filling out yet another application form fills students with dread. And why bother? Won't the same five or six kids who have been fighting over grade point averages since the fifth grade walk away with all the really good scholarships?

The truth is, most of the scholarships available to high school and college students are being offered because an organization wants to promote interest in a particular field, to encourage more students to become qualified to enter it, and finally, to help those students afford an education. Certainly, having a good grade point average is a valuable asset, and many organizations granting scholarships request that only applicants with a minimum grade point average apply. More often than not, however, grade point averages aren't even mentioned; the focus is on the area of interest and what a student has done to distinguish himself or herself in that area. In fact, frequently the only requirement is that the scholarship applicant must be studying in a particular area.

❏ GUIDELINES

When applying for scholarships, there are a few simple guidelines that can help ease the process considerably.

Plan Ahead

The absolute worst thing you can do is wait until the last minute. For one thing, obtaining recommendations or other supporting data in time to meet an application deadline is incredibly difficult. For another, no one does his or her best thinking or writing under the gun. So get off to a good start by reviewing scholarship applications as early as possible—months, even a year, in advance. If the current scholarship information isn't available, ask for a copy of last year's. Once you have the scholarship information or application in hand, give it a thorough read. Try to determine how your experience or situation best fits into the scholarship, or if it even fits at all. Don't waste your time applying for a scholarship in literature if you couldn't finish *Great Expectations*.

If possible, research the award or scholarship, including past recipients and, where applicable, the person in whose name the scholarship is offered. Often, public safety scholarships are established to memorialize a firefighter or police officer who died in the line of duty or an individual who played a key role in a particular field, such as FBI Director J. Edgar Hoover. In those cases, try to get a feel for the spirit of the person's work. If you have any similar interests or experiences, don't hesitate to mention them.

Talk to others who received the scholarship, or to students currently studying in the area or field of interest in which the scholarship is offered, and try to gain insight into possible applications or work related to that field. When you're working on the essay asking why you want this scholarship, you'll be able to demonstrate that you have informed answers to the questions: "I would benefit from receiving this scholarship because studying intelligence and a foreign language will help me to protect the United States from terrorism."

Take your time writing the essays. Be certain you are answering the question or questions on the application and not merely restating facts about yourself. Don't be afraid to get creative; try to imagine what you would think of if you had to sift through hundreds of applications. What would you want to know about the candidate? What would convince you that someone was deserving of the scholarship? Work through several drafts and have someone whose advice you respect—a parent, teacher, or guidance counselor—review the essay for grammar and content.

Finally, if you know in advance which scholarships you want to apply for, there might still be time to stack the deck in your favor by getting an internship, volunteering, or working part time. Bottom line: the more you know about a scholarship and the sooner you learn it, the better.

Follow Directions

Many of the organizations that offer scholarships devote 99.9 percent of their time to something other than the scholarship for which you are applying. Don't make a nuisance of yourself by pestering them for information. Simply follow the directions you are given. If the scholarship information specifies that you should write for information, then write for it—don't call.

Pay close attention to whether you're applying for an award, a scholarship, a prize, or financial aid. Often these words are used interchangeably, but just as often they have different meanings. An award is usually given for something you have done: built a park or helped distribute meals to the elderly; or something you have created: a design, an essay, a short film, a screenplay, an invention. On the other hand, a scholarship is frequently a renewable sum of money that is given to a person to defray the costs of college. Scholarships are given to candidates who meet the necessary criteria based on essays, eligibility, grades, and sometimes all three.

Supply all the necessary documents, information, and fees, and make the deadlines. You won't win any scholarships by forgetting to include a recommendation from your teacher or failing to postmark the application by the deadline. Bottom line: Get it right the first time, on time.

Apply Early

Once you have the application in hand, don't dawdle. If you've requested it far enough in advance, there shouldn't be any reason for you not to turn it in well before the deadline. You never know, if it comes down to two candidates, your timeliness just might be the deciding factor. Bottom line: Don't wait, don't hesitate.

Be Yourself

Don't make promises you can't keep. There are plenty of hefty scholarships available, but if they all require you to study something that you don't enjoy, you'll be miserable in college. And the side effects from switching majors after you've accepted a scholarship could be even worse. Bottom line: Be yourself.

Don't Limit Yourself

There are many sources for scholarships, beginning with your guidance counselor and ending with the Internet. All of the search engines have education categories. Start there and search by keywords, such as "financial aid," "scholarship," and "award." But don't be limited to the scholarships listed in these pages.

If you know of an organization related to or involved with the field of your choice, write a letter asking if they offer scholarships. If they don't offer scholarships, don't stop there. Write them another letter, or better yet, schedule a meeting with the president or someone in the public relations office and ask them if they would be willing to sponsor a scholarship for you. Of course, you'll need to prepare yourself well for such a meeting because you're selling a priceless commodity—yourself. Don't be shy, and be confident. Tell them all about yourself, what you want to study and why,

and let them know what you would be willing to do in exchange—volunteer at their favorite charity, write up reports on your progress in school, work part time on school breaks, or work full time during the summer. Explain why you're a wise investment. Bottom line: The sky's the limit.

❏ THE LIST
Air Force ROTC
Scholarship Actions Branch
551 East Maxwell Boulevard
Maxwell AFB, AL 36112-5917
866-423-7682
http://www.afrotc.com

The Air Force ROTC provides a wide range of four-year scholarships (partial or full tuition) to high school students planning to study foreign language, military justice, military arts and sciences, or other majors in college. Scholarships are also available to college and enlisted students. Visit the Air Force ROTC Web site to apply.

Alaska State Troopers
Division of Operations
Recruitment Supervisor
5700 East Tudor Road
Anchorage, AK 99507-1225
907-269-5759
http://alaskadvantage.state.ak.us/page/

The Michael Murphy Education Loan Fund provides loans of up to $1,000 per year to selected applicants who wish to pursue a certificate or degree in law enforcement, probation, or a closely related area. To qualify, students must be accepted into or already studying at an accredited college, be pursuing their studies full time, and have lived in Alaska for at least two years immediately prior to application. To maintain their yearly awards and to have their awards renewed, recipients must meet certain standards of academic achievement and residency requirements. Recipients of this funding may repay it in cash or have one-fifth of the debt forgiven for each year they work in law enforcement in Alaska.

American Legion Auxiliary

777 North Meridian Street,
    Third Floor
Indianapolis, IN 46204
317-955-3845
alahq@legion-aux.org
http://www.legion-aux.org/
    scholarships/index.aspx

State auxiliaries of the American Legion often offer scholarships to help students prepare for various careers. Most require that candidates be associated with the organization in some way, whether as a child or spouse, of a military veteran. Interested students should contact the American Legion Auxiliary for further information.

American Police Hall of Fame and Museum

American Police Hall of Fame
    Educational Scholarship Fund
3801 Biscayne Boulevard
Miami, FL 33137
policeinfo@aphf.org
http://www.aphf.org/scholarships.html

The American Police Hall of Fame Educational Scholarship Fund provides scholarships of $1,500 per year (up to four years) for college education to children of officers killed in the line of duty. Contact the American Police Hall of Fame and Museum for more information.

American Society of Criminology

1314 Kinnear Road
Columbus, OH 43212-1156
614-292-9207
http://www.asc41.com

The society offers the Minority Scholars/Mentors Research Grant Program for undergraduate students from underrepresented groups. Applicants must be near the end of their sophomore year of college to apply. Grantees receive $10,000, funds for travel to society meetings, guidance in the development of a research paper on a topic in criminology, guidance in the scholarly area of criminology, and assistance in applying for graduate school. Contact the society for further information and the name of the current Program chair.

Army ROTC

800-USA-ROTC
http://www.goarmy.com/rotc/
    scholarships.jsp

Students planning to pursue or currently pursuing a bachelor's degree may apply for scholarships that pay tuition and some living expenses; recipients must agree to accept a commission and serve in the army on Active Duty or in a Reserve Component (U.S. Army Reserve or Army

National Guard). Army career options include intelligence officer, police officer, and medical corps officer.

Association of Former Intelligence Officers (AFIO)
Attn: Scholarships Committee
6723 Whittier Avenue, Suite 303A
McLean, VA 22101-4533
afio@afio.com
http://www.afio.com/sections/ academic/scholarship.html

The association offers several scholarships to undergraduate and graduate students who are studying intelligence, international relations, foreign affairs, and/or national security studies. Applicants must be U.S. citizens and be attending a postsecondary institution in the United States. Contact the Scholarships Committee for more information.

Association on American Indian Affairs (AAIA)
Attn: Scholarship Coordinator
966 Hungerford Drive, Suite 12-B
Rockville, MD 20850-1743
240-314-7155
general.aaia@verizon.net
http://www.indian-affairs.org

Native American undergraduate and graduate students who are pursuing a wide variety of college majors (including criminal justice and health care) can apply for several different scholarships ranging from $500 to $1,500. All applicants must provide proof of Native American heritage. Visit the association's Web site for more information.

Central Intelligence Agency (CIA)
Undergraduate Scholarship Program
http://www.cia.gov/employment/ student.html#usp

High school seniors and college sophomores who are planning to enroll or who are currently enrolled in college are eligible for up to $18,000 per school year for tuition, fees, books, and supplies. Applicants must be at least 18 years of age by April 1 of the year of application, be U.S. citizens, demonstrate financial need, have a minimum score of 1000 on the SAT or 21 on the ACT, and be willing to relocate to the Washington, D.C., area for summer employment. Scholars selected for the program must agree to continue employment with the agency in the Washington, D.C., area after college graduation for a period 1.5 times the length of their college scholarships. Although the Undergraduate Scholarship Program was developed specifically for minority students and students with disabilities, it is open to all students.

CollegeBoard.com
http://apps.collegeboard.com/ cbsearch_ss/welcome.jsp

This testing service (PSAT, SAT, etc.) offers a scholarship search engine that features scholarships (not all safety- and security-related) worth nearly $3 billion. You can search by specific major and a variety of other criteria.

CollegeNET
http://mach25.collegenet.com/cgi- bin/M25/index

CollegeNET features 600,000 scholarships (not all safety- and security-related) worth more than $1.6 billion. You can search by keywords (such as "criminal justice") or by creating a personality profile of your interests.

Daughters of the American Revolution (DAR)
Attn: Scholarship Committee
1776 D Street NW
Washington, DC 20006-5303
202-628-1776
http://www.dar.org/natsociety/
    edout_scholar.cfm

General scholarships are available to students who have been accepted by or who are currently enrolled in a college or university in the United States. Selection criteria include academic excellence, commitment to field of study, and financial need; applicants need not be affiliated with DAR. A scholarship program is also available for Native American students. Contact the Scholarship Committee for more information.

FastWeb
http://fastweb.monster.com

FastWeb features 600,000 scholarships (not all safety and security related) worth more than $1 billion. To use this resource, you will need to register (free).

Foundation for the Carolinas
PO Box 34769
Charlotte, NC 28234-4769
704-973-4500
infor@fftc.org
http://www.fftc.org

The foundation administers more than 70 scholarship funds that offer awards to undergraduate and graduate students pursuing study in law enforcement and other fields. Visit its Web site for a searchable list of awards.

Golden Key International Honour Society
621 North Avenue NE, Suite C-100
Atlanta, GA 30308-2842
800-377-2401
memberservices@goldenkey.org
http://www.goldenkey.org/GKWeb

Golden Key is an academic honor society that offers its members "opportunities for individual growth through leadership, career development, networking, and service." It awards more than $400,000 in scholarships annually through 17 different award programs. Membership in the society is selective; only the top 15 percent of college juniors and seniors—who may be pursuing education in any college major—are considered for membership by the organization. There is a one-time membership fee of $70. Contact the society for more information.

GuaranteedScholarships.com
http://www.guaranteed-scholarships.
    com

This Web site offers lists (by college) of scholarships, grants, and financial aid (not all safety- and security-related) that "require no interview, essay, portfolio, audition, competition, or other secondary requirement."

Hispanic College Fund (HCF)

1717 Pennsylvania Avenue NW,
  Suite 460
Washington, DC 20006-4629
hcf-info@hispanicfund.org
http://www.hispanicfund.org

The Hispanic College Fund, in collaboration with several major corporations, offers a variety of scholarships for high school seniors and college students planning to attend or currently attending college. Applicants must be Hispanic, live in the United States or Puerto Rico, and have a GPA of at least 3.0 on a 4.0 scale. Contact the HCF for more information.

Illinois Career Resource Network

http://www.ilworkinfo.com/icrn.htm

Created by the Illinois Department of Employment Security, this useful site offers a great scholarship search engine, as well as detailed information on careers (including those in safety and security). You can search for scholarships by major (such as criminology, criminal justice, fire science and firefighting, fire protection, and emergency medical care) or other keywords. This site is available to everyone, not just Illinois residents; you can get a password by simply visiting the site. The Illinois Career Information System is just one example of sites created by state departments of employment security (or departments of labor) to assist students with financial and career-related issues. After checking out this site, visit the Web site of your state's department of labor to see what it offers.

International Association of Arson Investigators Educational Foundation

12772 Boenker Road
Bridgeton, MO 63044-2436
314-739-4224
http://www.firearson.com/ef/
  jcwscholar/app.asp

Students currently studying or planning to study fire science, law enforcement, fire and arson investigation, prelaw, or forensic science are eligible to apply for the John Charles Wilson Scholarship. Applicants must submit certified academic transcripts and an essay of no more than 500 words that details their background and professional plans upon graduation. Contact the foundation for more information.

International Association of Firefighters (IAFF)

W. H. "Howie" McClennan
  Scholarship
Office of the General President
1750 New York Avenue NW
Washington, DC 20006
202-737-8484
http://www.iaff.org/academy/
  scholarships/mcclennan.html

Sons, daughters, or legally adopted children of firefighters killed in the line of duty who are planning to attend college may apply for the $2,500 W. H. "Howie" McClennan Scholarship. Scholarships are awarded based on financial need, aptitude, promise, and academic achievement. Contact the Office of the General President for more information.

International Union of Police Associations, AFL-CIO

Attn: Scholarship Program
1549 Ringling Boulevard, Suite 600
Sarasota, FL 34236-6772
iupa@iupa.org
http://www.iupa.org

This union for law enforcement and law enforcement support personnel offers the Edward J. Kiernan Memorial Scholarship to children of its members who are pursuing postsecondary education. Contact the union for more information.

J. Edgar Hoover Foundation

Attn: Chairman
PO Box 5914
Hilton Head, SC 29938-5914
il@jedgarhooverfoundation.org
http://www.jedgarhooverfoundation.
    org/scholar/scholar.html

Undergraduate and graduate students who demonstrate financial need may apply for J. Edgar Hoover Foundation Scholarships, which range from $500 to $1,000 annually. Visit the foundation's Web site to download an application. J. Edgar Hoover was the director of the Federal Bureau of Investigation for nearly 50 years.

Marine Corps Scholarship Foundation

PO Box 3008
Princeton, NJ 08543-3008
800-292-7777
mcsf@marine-scholars.org
http://www.marine-scholars.org

The foundation helps children of marines and former marines with scholarships of up to $5,000 for study in a variety of fields. To be eligible, you must be a high school graduate or registered as an undergraduate student at an accredited college or vo-tech institute. Additionally, your total family gross income may not exceed $61,000. Contact the foundation for further details.

National Black Police Association (NBPA)

Attn: Scholarship Committee
3251 Mount Pleasant Street NW,
    2nd Floor
Washington, DC 20010-2103
202-986-2070
http://www.blackpolice.org

The Alphonso Deal Scholarship Award is presented by the National Black Police Association to a high school senior who wishes to study law enforcement or a closely related field at a two- or four-year college. Applicants must be U.S. citizens and accepted into their college of choice. The scholarship is awarded on the basis of academic achievement, recommendations, and character. The amount of the award is at the discretion of the National Black Police Association's Scholarship Committee.

National Fire Protection Association (NFPA)

NFPA Fire Safety Educational
    Memorial Fund
Attn: Christine Ellis
One Batterymarch Park
Quincy, MA 02169-7471
617-770-3000
http://www.nfpa.org

The association offers several scholarships to undergraduate and graduate students who are pursuing study in fire protection engineering, fire science, and/or public administration. Visit the association's Web site for details on specific scholarships and to download applications.

National Security Agency (NSA)
9800 Savage Road, Suite 6779
Ft. George G. Meade, MD 20755-6779
866-672-4473
http://www.nsa.gov/careers/
  students_4.cfm

Undergraduate and graduate students who plan to pursue careers in intelligence, global networking, or language analysis upon graduation may apply for the Pat Roberts Intelligence Scholars Program. Contact the NSA for more information.

National Sheriffs' Association (NSA)
Attn: Tim Woods, NSA Scholarship
  Program
1450 Duke Street
Alexandria, VA 22314-3490
703-836-7827
http://www.sheriffs.org/nsa-
  scholarship.shtml

Students who are planning to major or currently majoring in criminal justice or a related field in an undergraduate or graduate college program may apply for NSA Scholarships of $1,000. Applicants must work for a sheriff's office or be the child of an individual employed by a sheriff's office. Visit the association's Web site to download an application.

Navy: Education: Earn Money For College
http://www.navy.com/education/
  earnmoneyforcollege

The Navy offers several funding programs for college study. Students who receive money to attend college are typically required to serve a specific number of years in the Navy after graduation. Other students take advantage of programs that allow them to join the Navy and complete their degrees during their service obligation. Contact your local recruiter or visit the Navy's Web site for details.

Sallie Mae
http://www.collegeanswer.com/index.
  jsp

This Web site offers a scholarship database of more than 2.4 million awards (not all safety- and security-related) worth more than $14 billion. You must register (free) to use the database.

Scholarship America
1 Scholarship Way
St. Peter, MN 56082-1693
800-537-4180
http://www.scholarshipamerica.org

This organization works through its local Dollars for Scholars chapters in 41 states and the District of Columbia. In 2003, it awarded more than $29 million in scholarships to students. Visit Scholarship America's Web site for more information.

Scholarships.com
http://www.scholarships.com

Scholarships.com offers a free college scholarship search engine (although you must register to use it) and financial aid information.

Texas Sheriff's Association Scholarship

Attn: Scholarship Program
1601 South IH 35
Austin, TX 78741-2503
http://www.txsheriffs.org

The association offers several scholarships to college undergraduate and graduate students. Applicants must have a GPA of at least 2.5, be less than 25 years of age at the time of application, and have completed at least one semester of college. They must also submit a brief biographical sketch and narrative. Contact the association for more information.

United Negro College Fund (UNCF)

http://www.uncf.org/scholarships

Visitors to the UNCF Web site can search for thousands of scholarships and grants, many of which are administered by the UNCF. High school seniors and undergraduate and graduate students are eligible. The search engine allows you to search by major, state, scholarship title, grade level, and achievement score.

Look to the Pros

The following professional organizations offer a variety of materials, from career brochures to lists of accredited schools to salary surveys. Many also publish journals and newsletters that you should become familiar with. Some have annual conferences that you might be able to attend. (While you may not be able to attend a conference as a participant, it may be possible to cover one for your school or even your local paper, especially if your school has a related club.)

When contacting professional organizations, keep in mind that they all exist primarily to serve their members, be it through continuing education, professional licensure, political lobbying, or just keeping up with the profession. While many are strongly interested in promoting their profession and providing information about it to the general public, these professional organizations are busy with many other activities. Whether you call or write, be courteous, brief, and to the point. Know what you need and ask for it. If the organization has a Web site, check it out first: what you're looking for may be available there for downloading, or you may find a list of prices or instructions, such as sending a self-addressed stamped envelope with your request. Finally, be aware that organizations, like people, move. To save time when writing, first confirm the address, preferably with a quick phone call to the organization itself: "Hello, I'm calling to confirm your address. . . ."

Alpha Group Center for Crime and Intelligence Analysis (AGC)
PO Box 8
Montclair, CA 91763-0008
909-476-7281
crimecrush@aol.com
http://www.alphagroupcenter.com

Contact the Alpha Group for a schedule of courses in crime analysis, investigative analysis, and intelligence analysis throughout the United States and Canada.

American Correctional Association (ACA)
4380 Forbes Boulevard
Lanham, MD 20706-4322
301-918-1800
http://www.aca.org

Contact the ACA for information on job openings, certification, and corrections-related Web sites, books, and periodicals.

American Jail Association (AJA)
1135 Professional Court
Hagerstown, MD 21740-5853
301-790-3930
http://www.corrections.com/aja/
    index.shtml

Contact the AJA for information on careers in corrections, certification, and student membership.

American Police Hall of Fame and Museum

6350 Horizon Drive
Titusville, FL 32780-8002
321-264-0911
policeinfo@aphf.org
http://www.aphf.org/museum.html

Created by the American Federation of Police and Concerned Citizens and the National Association of Chiefs of Police, the American Police Hall of Fame and Museum offers summer camps, scholarships, and other information for young people interested in police work.

American Probation and Parole Association

2760 Research Park Drive
Lexington, KY 40511-8410
859-244-8203
appa@csg.org
http://www.appa-net.org

This is a professional organization for probation, parole, and community corrections professionals. Visit its Web site to learn about issues affecting workers in the field.

American Society of Criminology (ASC)

1314 Kinnear Road
Columbus, OH 43212-1156
614-292-9207
http://www.asc41.com

Contact the ASC for information on careers in criminology. The society also offers a Minority Scholars/Mentors Research Grant program for undergraduate students from underrepresented groups and an e-mail mentoring program.

Association of Former Intelligence Officers (AFIO)

6723 Whittier Avenue, Suite 303A
McLean, VA 22101-4533
703-790-0320
afio@afio.com
http://www.afio.com

This is an organization of former intelligence officials in the CIA, the FBI, other federal and state government departments, and law enforcement entities. Contact the AFIO for information about scholarships for undergraduate and graduate students and a list of members willing to speak at schools.

Federal Bureau of Investigation (FBI)

Personnel Resources Office
J. Edgar Hoover Building
935 Pennsylvania Avenue NW
Washington, DC 20535-0001
202-324-3000
http://www.fbi.gov and http://www.fbi.gov/fbikids.htm

Contact the FBI for information on a career as an FBI agent, internships for undergraduate and graduate students, advice on landing a job at the FBI, and FBI Citizens' Academies (for people age 21 and over).

Federal Bureau of Prisons (BOP)

320 First Street NW
Washington, DC 20534-0002
http://www.bop.gov

Contact the BOP for information on entrance requirements, training, and career opportunities for corrections officers at the federal level.

International Association of Arson Investigators

12770 Boenker Road
Bridgeton, MO 63044-2436
314-739-4224
http://www.firearson.com

Contact the association for information on arson investigation and scholarships for undergraduate students.

International Association of Chiefs of Police (IACP)

515 North Washington Street
Alexandria, VA 22314
703-836-6767
information@theiacp.org
http://www.theiacp.org

The IACP is a professional membership organization for police chiefs, commissioners, sheriffs, constables, security officers, investigators, colonels, city managers, public safety directors, instructors, highway safety specialists, police science coordinators, brigadier generals, doctors, senior research fellows, sergeants, criminal investigators, psychologists, attorneys, management analysts, border patrol agents, inspectors, human rights officers, coroners, and handwriting examiners. It publishes *Police Chief* magazine.

International Association of Crime Analysts

9218 Metcalf Avenue, #364
Overland Park, KS 66212-1476
800-609-3419
http://www.iaca.net

Contact the association for information on careers, job listings, certification, e-mail listservs related to crime analysis, and useful articles and publications.

International Association of Fire Chiefs

4025 Fair Ridge Drive, Suite 300
Fairfax, VA 22033-2868
703-273-0911
http://www.iafc.org

Visit the association's Web site to read about issues that affect fire chiefs.

International Association of Firefighters

1750 New York Avenue NW
Washington, DC 20006
202-737-8484
http://www.iaff.org

This labor union for firefighters provides information on earnings and scholarships to undergraduate students. It also publishes *International Fire Fighter*.

International Association of Women Police (IAWP)

PO Box 690418
Tulsa, OK 74169-0418
918-234-6445
http://www.iawp.org

Contact this organization for information on career opportunities in policing for women.

International Union of Police Associations, AFL-CIO

1549 Ringling Boulevard, Suite 600
Sarasota, FL 34236
iupa@iupa.org
http://www.iupa.org

The International Union of Police Associations is a union for law enforcement
and law enforcement support personnel. Visit its Web site for information on
scholarships and union activities.

Law Enforcement Association of Asian Pacifics (LEAAP)

905 East Second Street, Suite 200
Los Angeles, CA 90012-4319
amerasia@starmail.com
http://members.tripod.com/
   ~amerasia2

This is a professional association of Asian
Pacific law enforcement officers in federal, municipal, state, county, and other
agencies.

National Association of Emergency Medical Technicians (NAEMT)

PO Box 1400
Clinton, MS 39060-1400
800-346-2368
info@naemt.org
http://www.naemt.org

Contact the association for job listings and
information on student membership.

National Association of Police Organizations

750 First Street NE, Suite 920
Washington, DC 20002-8005
202-842-4420
info@napo.org
http://www.napo.org

The National Association of Police Organizations is a coalition of police unions
and associations that work to advance

the interests of law enforcement officers
through legislation, political action, and
education.

National Black Police Association (NBPA)

3251 Mount Pleasant Street NW,
   2nd Floor
Washington, DC 20010-2103
202-986-2070
http://www.blackpolice.org

This professional organization represents
the interests of African-Americans in law
enforcement. Visit its Web site for job
listings and information on scholarships.

National Fire Protection Association

One Batterymarch Park
Quincy, MA 02169-7471
617-770-3000
http://www.nfpa.org

This organization offers fact sheets and
statistics on fires, job listings, public education programs, and financial aid for
undergraduate and graduate students.

National Organization of Black Law Enforcement Executives

4609 Pinecrest Office Park Drive,
   Suite F
Alexandria, VA 22312-1442
703-658-1529
noble@noblenatl.org
http://www.noblenatl.org

The membership of this professional organization consists of African-American
police chiefs, sheriffs, command-level officers, and others. It conducts research,

speaks out on issues affecting the African-American community, and performs a variety of outreach activities.

National Registry of Emergency Medical Technicians

Rocco V. Morando Building
PO Box 29233
6610 Busch Boulevard
Columbus, OH 43229-0233
614-888-4484
http://www.nremt.org

Contact this organization for information on EMT certification tests.

National Sheriffs' Association

1450 Duke Street
Alexandria, VA 22314-3490
703-836-7827
http://www.sheriffs.org

This professional organization for sheriffs publishes *Sheriff* magazine and the *Sheriffs' Directory*. It also provides a scholarship to those planning to or currently attending an undergraduate or graduate academic institution.

Society of Fire Protection Engineers

7315 Wisconsin Avenue, Suite 620E
Bethesda, MD 20814-3234
301-718-2910
sfpehqtrs@sfpe.org
http://www.sfpe.org

The society provides detailed information on fire protection engineering careers at its Web site. It also offers free electronic membership to students.

Transportation Security Administration (TSA)

601 South 12th Street
Arlington, VA 22202-4220
http://www.tsa.gov

The TSA is responsible for the security of transportation systems in the United States. Visit its Web site for career information, details on the nation's threat advisory level, and tips on flying and packing safely.

U.S. Citizenship and Immigration Services (USCIS)

http://uscis.gov/graphics/index.htm

Visit the USCIS Web site for information on applying for employment, plus a list of frequently asked questions and answers.

U.S. Fire Administration

16825 South Seton Avenue
Emmitsburg, MD 21727-8920
301-447-1000
http://www.usfa.fema.gov

The administration offers information about national fire programs, statistics on firefighting, and details about the National Fire Academy.

U.S. Secret Service

245 Murray Drive, Building 410
Washington, DC 20223
202-406-5800
http://www.secretservice.gov

To learn about careers, download employment applications, and read frequently asked questions, visit the Secret Service's Web site.

Index

Entries and page numbers in **bold** indicate major treatment of a topic.